Secrets From My
Travel Diaries

Secrets From My Travel Diaries
How One Burnt Out Executive
Reignited the Adventurer Within

Stacey L. Abella

Published by Game Changer Publishing

Paperback ISBN: 978-1-961189-03-4
Hardcover ISBN: 978-1-961189-04-1
Digital ISBN: 978-1-961189-05-8

www.GameChangerPublishing.com

Dedication

To Mom and Dad, who encouraged me to go where they'd never been.

Read This First

Just to say thanks for buying and reading my book, I would like to give you a few free bonus gifts, no strings attached!

To Download Your Free Gifts Now, Visit:
http://Igniteyouradventurer.com/bookfreegifts

Secrets From My Travel Diaries

How One Burnt Out Executive
Reignited the Adventurer Within

Stacey L. Abella

 **GAME CHANGER** PUBLISHING

www.GameChangerPublishing.com

Table of Contents

Introduction

It's taken so much more than I ever imagined to co-write this book with my 21-year-old self: to see myself for who I thought I was, who I am now, and who I can be. I've preserved the diaries' voice and spirit to tell the story how I saw it then, while also capturing the raw emotions of today.

I invite you to flip through the handwritten pages with me; to travel to places far and near; to step back into what's past, and find your possibility.

Even if you feel off-course, I hope that you will see a pathway to the life you always wanted – the one you always thought you'd have – and still can.

It's time to connect to the Adventurer inside you. Clear the decks. Point your compass in a new direction. Take the helm. Catch the wind.

Hop aboard — let's go!

Preface
Back to the Source

September 2, 2021

I'm sitting here, alone in my house on Tuesday morning. It seems like years that I've been yearning for one day – just one day – to be free from the things that I always have to do.

And now here I am. Yesterday I said goodbye to my team at work.

I don't even know how to feel right now.

Words. …. The deluge of them pulls me onto my couch. I grab my phone and start to dictate into it.

I'm writing in the third person about a phantom "she." Her name is similar to mine, but not the same.

Anastasia. That's what I name her.

It's the name I wished my parents had given me when I was a kid. During roll call on that first day of school, I longed to hear my teacher read out "Anastasia" from the roster.

Then I'd say, "That's my real name, but I go by Stacey." Just like the others in my class who went by something different, like "Ben," "Jenny," and "Thomas."

The "Anastasia" I'm writing about is a high-powered career woman. She gets dangerously burned out, is forced to slow down – and realizes she doesn't even know what happened to the last ten-plus years.

"She got what she thought she wanted – and it wasn't what she wanted," I type onto the screen.

I keep writing about how she's been running on a treadmill, the belt cycling round and round. Eventually, she can't keep up the pace anymore.

Like me… Like the clients that I coach in the side business I am turning into full-time… Like a lot of people I know.

This Anastasia I'm writing about is lost …

She's lost in her work… In her responsibilities… In other people's expectations…

Who is she?
Who am I?
Where do I go from here?

September 29, 2021

The words are pouring out like a fountain, like pent-up pressure breaking free, bringing into the light what was hidden below the surface.

I'm writing about all the things that Anastasia is realizing about her life… How she's been chasing the wind… How she forgot where she was going and why.

But that's Anastasia's story. What about mine?

I guess I'm not who I used to be, either. Or am I?

1997. 21 years old. My study abroad in Europe. Those were the days!

Writing a book about that pivotal time in my life has dwelled in the back of my mind for years. What did it all mean?

I've started writing about the places I've been and what I remember.

But the memories have become muted, grayed out, dim. They yield no answers.

I still have all those diaries, though. What's even in them?

October 5, 2021

I've been trying to write about going to the wrong city in Germany. There were two cities with almost exactly the same name.

I thought I knew what they were called.

But the search bar isn't working. I'm not asking the right questions, I guess. I'm not close enough to key in on the right thing.

Again and again, I keep returning random things. That's still not it. . .

My diaries. The answers are in my diaries.

I guess it's the only way I'm going to find those names.

I know those diaries are up there. They're in one of those storage boxes in my closet that have moved with me wherever I've gone. I haven't opened them in years.

One of them has that famous cathedral in Florence on the cover. I bought it there and wrote in it on the train on the way back to Freiburg. . .

October 6, 2021

I found the diary with the Florence cover on a shelf in my closet. There were three others, too, collecting dust in a box above my business suits. I think of going in there every day to select something to wear, with those the dairies lying in wait above me.

It's kind of eerie looking at them. My handwriting is different now, but also kind of the same.

I definitely wrote a lot more neatly then. The years of computers and phones have gotten me out of practice, writing by hand with paper and pen.

It would take me a long time to write a single sentence that neatly now. Let alone fill up four whole diaries – on moving trains.

I flip through the first one, and these words catch my eye: *"I want to grasp onto these fleeting, wonderful moments because never again will I be this free."*

A prickle of knowing bristles through me. From somewhere deep inside, those words strike a chord of familiarity. Have they been painted on the walls of my mind ever since?

After getting lost in reading for a while, I stagger stiffly from the floor of my closet, gather up the diaries, and shake out my legs that have fallen asleep.

I go to my computer and get transported back in time some more. Then, I hit the microphone. My handwritten words begin to track across the computer screen…

They rewind all the years and land on February 18, 1997.

That was the day before we left for Freiburg. The story weaves onto the computer screen...

February 18, 1997

Tomorrow, I'm going to Europe to study abroad in Freiburg, Germany, in the southern part of Germany called the *Schwarzwald* [Black Forest]. The adventure doesn't really start tomorrow, though. Like anything else, it started much earlier – with a thought and a dream. I'm going to call the beginning *dish duty*.

Dish duty was my brainy idea to make money for our Eurail passes. My friend Clarissa, who is also going to Freiburg, was up for doing dish duty, too, which was great because some of those dishes were really dicey.

Every weekday of the semester, we'd wash dishes at our sorority house. And thirty sorority sisters generate a lot of dirty dishes!

On Mondays, the crusty weekend dishes would emerge from the corners of people's rooms. We'd find them beneath the fresh mound of plates and pots and pans from Monday's lunch. The worst seemed to be the melted-cheese remains from weekend snacks.

The dirty dishes didn't phase us much, though. We knew those dishes were getting us to Europe and that every last one was bringing us closer to freedom, adventure, and the realization of a dream.

The University of Freiburg, Germany, was our jumping-off point. The Eurail passes we bought, thanks to those dishes, would take us wherever we wanted to go.

Herr Daly, our German professor, said that every time he saw Clarissa and me, we were always laughing. I guess that's true. Laughter got us through the stacks of dishes – and a lot of other challenges, too.

One night after dinner at the sorority house, Clarissa and I lingered long after everyone had gone. We brainstormed the countries to visit in random order: Germany, France, Switzerland, Italy, Spain, Austria, The Netherlands, Belgium, Sweden, Denmark, and Hungary.

The university town of Freiburg, where we're going, is pretty much in the middle of Europe, near the borders of France and Switzerland. It's the perfect jumping-off point to anywhere we want to go.

A single hole punch on our Eurail passes would kick off an entire 24 hours of travel. Who knew what awaited out there on the open horizon? We'd be as free as we'd ever be …

Secrets From My Travel Diaries

> ➤ *Crusty dishes aren't so bad... When you can laugh with a friend – and when you know why you're washing them.*

PART 1

STEPPING OUT

CHAPTER 1

Never Again Will You Be This Free

"Now, as I look ahead into the Unknown, I know that this time will be what I make it … and I'm all set to make it all that I want it to be."

February 19, 1997

I'm opening the page of a brand-new diary – hopefully filled with all kinds of new and exciting adventures. This one finds Clarissa and me finally in the air on our way to Germany.

Part of me feels as though this day took forever to arrive. In another nagging corner of my mind is a frightened little girl, crying that this moment has arrived too soon. One way or another, I'm somewhere over the middle of the Atlantic, and there's no turning back now.

Before I left, Dad and I talked about what lay ahead for me in these months abroad, and he encouraged me to embrace the opportunity. He reminded me that never again would I find myself this free – to travel, and do whatever I want, and go wherever the wind might blow.

By American standards, after graduation next year, I have to go out and start my career and make something of myself. Sometimes, I wish we were more like the Europeans, who seem to be able to travel around and "sow their wild oats" before even thinking of getting a job. There is a lot we could learn from other cultures, I believe.

When I think of the European exchange students I've met in the U.S., I feel silly to be making a big deal out of being away from home for a mere six months. But on the other hand, I know that what Clarissa and I are doing is rather uncommon for our culture, though perhaps less so in our generation.

For now, though, going to Europe is somewhere I feel I need to go. I'm scared for what awaits me on the other side of this flight, but I also know that all wonderful new things in life come with a little fear mixed in. It's worth feeling that fear in exchange for gaining the experience.

Yesterday I met up with Stephanie, my friend and mentor. As a farewell gift, she presented me with a beautiful card with a quote on it:

"Twenty years from now you will be more disappointed by the things you didn't do than by the ones you did. So, throw off the bowlines. Sail away from the safe harbor. Catch the trade winds in your sails. Explore. Dream. Discover."
– H. Jackson Brown Jr.

This is *my time* to run free with the wind, to learn about this culture and my own ability to adapt in it. At 21, I'm embarking on a journey to figure out who I am and to bask in the joy of being young and so alive. I truly hope these next six months will shape the rest of my life and that these moments will age into memories that I will cherish for a lifetime.

Worries beyond my control haunt me, though. If anything happened to anyone back home, I don't know what I would do. I want to embrace the newness of everything around me in Europe, but I also know that at some point, I have to find my way back to my loved ones and the life that I am leaving behind.

For now, this is my time to step out into the world. I have been to Europe before: on a high school trip through France when I was 16, and a summer program in Lutherstadt Wittenberg, Germany, during my first summer in college. What makes this time different is that I'm so much more on my own.

In Freiburg, it will be up to me to make my own class schedule, my own travel plans, and to make the experience what I want it to be. This is a stepping stone to life after I graduate – at least, that's the way I see it.

Studying abroad, traveling, and experiencing life on my terms is something I've wanted to do for a long time. Curiosity about what I don't understand has become a part of me. I want to enjoy every bit of this new freedom. At the same time, I want to learn to really understand – to see past the initial dazzle of newness to what is really there.

It's like the advice I got from a businessman who was sitting next to me on the plane from Cleveland. He saw me putting my big backpack in the overhead and asked me what I was planning to do in Europe. Then he proceeded to tell me all kinds of stories about traveling all over the world.

He warned me that it's easy to become fascinated and blinded by a person's uniqueness. But that fascination wears off, and you realize that there was no true substance beyond the shiny exterior.

If you don't see past that in time, you're "headed for an *international boo-boo*," he said. And he shared his story about living overseas and bringing someone back with him, only to realize when the dazzle wore off that he had had no idea who she even was. . .

We ended up talking to him for most of the flight, and he gave us his business card and asked us to send him a postcard. (Clarissa later told me she planned on saving her stamps for someone she actually knew, though, which made sense.) In any case, with his numerous international travels, he was interesting to talk to.

Time keeps ticking by so slowly. The unknown waits on the other side of this flight and is creeping up on me. It is a matter of hours before we land. I keep fighting with myself, trying to temper my ultra-high expectations so I don't get disappointed, yet still dreaming that my time in Europe will be better than I can even imagine.

I have *six months* until I return to the reality of duties and responsibilities … *six months*. It's so short in a lifetime but seems so long right now, with its open canvas stretching out before me.

As I write these words, I am imagining that someday, these diaries can become a novel. It is kind of a dream of mine to publish a book, so I can leave even a tiny mark on the world, made by the thoughts in my head.

Right now, though, I'm so tired. I want to try to get a little sleep, as uncomfortable as it is to be scrunched up in this seat.

February 19, 1997 – 12:15 PM

Somehow, we've made it this far. We are at last on the train to Freiburg. It has been far from easy. We didn't realize how good we had it when we studied in Germany two summers ago and got picked up right from the airport. This time when we arrived, we found ourselves completely on our own with our oversized suitcases, and still hours away from our destination.

At the baggage claim in Frankfurt, our bags came out right away – and then, we realized we had no idea what to do with them. We saw some carts but thought they required coins. So, for some reason we decided it would be easier to strap our four big suitcases together and drag them.

The tiny wheels of the suitcases barely rolled at all, and our luggage kept tipping over in a big mound. Finally, we figured out that the carts were free – and that we could take them all the way to the train station at the bottom of the airport.

We dragged our luggage down the station's escalator but could not find Freiburg on the sign. After much confusion, we wrestled the luggage back up again and found the ticket place. (At that point, we had gotten a little less awkward at hauling our luggage.)

At the ticket place, we ran into a student from Wisconsin who was joining our program, too. The airline lost all her luggage, so she had only her backpack and two free hands. Thanks to her and the others who helped us along the way, we have managed this far with our pile of heavy luggage.

On the train, we met a couple of Germans who happened to be going to Freiburg, too, and they instructed us where to go. We must have been a sight when we got off that train. As we were struggling to get our luggage out the door, one of the conductors yelled, *"Schneller! Schneller!" ["Faster! Faster!"]*. There wasn't much we could do to speed up, though.

When we finally got off the train, we realized we had gotten off on the wrong side and had to go up and down a big set of stairs to get across. Luckily, some guy helped us, or we'd probably still be there.

One way or another, we have a couple of hours until we arrive in Freiburg. There must be some easier way because this has been truly hell, breaking our backs over these bags. If I didn't think I'd need this stuff later, I'd be ready to leave one behind. We sure have made a grand entrance into this country we're about to call home… for now.

The ordeal we have been through, and the lack of sleep, have put everything into perspective for me, though. It feels like I left the ghosts of my past relationships, and everything else from my life in the U.S., somewhere on the drive to the Cleveland airport. I'm starting completely anew.

Now, as I look out the train window, this place looks like any other big city surrounding an airport. Only the German street signs indicate how far I've come. But somehow, I've stepped into a different world and a new life. Suddenly, home feels so very far away.

February 19, 1997 – 9 PM

It's still February 19th on this same incredibly long day. After a great deal of confusion, a feeling I'm quickly beginning to get sick of, I am sitting in my room in *Merzhauserstraße,* my apartment complex in Freiburg. It is a suite, which consists of five bedrooms, a hallway, and a kitchen. Right now, though, it's eerily quiet. The German students are on break, and there seems to be no one around.

Only serving to make me more disoriented, my bed has weird sheets, no pillow, and there are no blinds on my window. The pillowcase I brought from home serves no purpose until I can find a pillow. Until then, I'll use one of my thicker jackets as a substitute.

This is definitely a low point. After 30 or 40 hours of no sleep, what did I expect, though? Eventually, I keep telling myself, this will all become part of my "big adventure." When I look back, maybe I'll even remember it all fondly.

For now, though, I feel like I have so many questions unanswered. This perpetually lost feeling is weighing on my mind.

I couldn't even figure out how to call my parents. The phone makes weird noises, and I have no idea what to do.

Surely, things will get better.

My flatmates [roommates] will become soul mates, and at least a few of the 40 Americans in my program will be fun to travel with. (Maybe they'll even have a sense of direction, as I always struggle with that.)

I am beyond the point of exhaustion, so I will close this entry – still with hope, but with more than a few misgivings. This will be an adventure, all right.

February 21, 1997

A lot of random things have happened since the night and day since I last wrote. One of my flatmates showed up, and she seems really cool. She invited me to breakfast with some of her friends, but I couldn't go because I had to take a German placement test at the program office.

After the test, the group of 40 of us went on a tour of the city. The town of Freiburg looks quaint and beautiful and has a lot of places I'd love to check out. I'm still really disoriented in directions, though, and have no idea how I'll find those places again.

During the city tour, I hung out with Clarissa, these two guys named Mike and Tom, and another student named Anne. Mike was assigned to the same five-person suite as Clarissa. He and Tom know each other from school, the same as Clarissa and me. Anne lives in the same apartment building, too, and seems like a lot of fun.

After the tour, we had lunch at the university *Mensa* [cafeteria]. The trays of food were spat out of a conveyor, each one identical. We each managed to get a hold of a tray of food before the conveyor whisked it away.

Buying a drink was the next ordeal. I successfully bought one from the vending machine but couldn't figure out how to open the bottle. Eventually, as a line was forming behind me, I slinked back to the table, feeling embarrassed.

A rather good-looking German guy sat down next to Clarissa and me. He asked us what was wrong, and when we told him, he gallantly proceeded to open our bottles with his fork. The bottle tops arched up, ricocheting backward toward the table behind us. I was amazed that the woman eating there didn't even look up as the bottle tops sailed past her head.

The bottle-opening started a conversation about where we were from and when we'd arrived. He encouraged us by saying that it was *ganz normal* [totally normal] to feel lost and confused in the beginning. Somehow, that didn't really help, but it was fun to have our first real conversation in German at the university.

After lunch, a group of us went to the grocery store with one of the full-year students. She showed us the cheapest things to cook on a student budget and where to go.

At the grocery store, a guy came up to one of the students in our group and started asking her if she was having difficulty picking out butter. He proceeded to give her a tour of all the butter available, conducted in English, with us trying not to crack up.

Afterward, we went to Woolworth's to get speakers for our Walkmans because we can't live without music, and there's no other way to play it.

February 22, 1997

Today, I had only one mishap: I got on the *Straßenbahn* [streetcar] going the wrong direction. I managed to notice after a few stops. Trying to seem cool and collected, I got off at the nearest stop as nonchalantly as possible and walked across the street to catch the streetcar going the opposite direction.

I don't know if it's jet lag or what, but I have this spacy, tired feeling that I can't shake. As of today, I still have no pillow, and the sheets that are too short are a constant battle at night. Still, my bed is somehow so incredibly comfortable, maybe just because I'm so tired.

We have met a lot of cool people from the program. What we're all going through together seems to have created such a bond, even though I've only known them for a few days. We've been having an especially good time with Mike and Tom, the guys I mentioned earlier (although their sense of direction seems to be as bad as ours).

Somehow, every day here seems like a month. I guess it's because of everything that is going on around me, this new life I'm living, and all these experiences that I can't even begin to explain to my friends at home.

Yesterday must have been eons ago, according to the time warp I'm in now. I know that things will pick up eventually, though – especially in a few weeks when we wrap up our language immersion and classes start for the semester.

February 23, 1997

I'm out on my balcony right now, looking out at the mountains in the distance. There are a bunch of people playing soccer beneath my window. Soon, the air will get cooler, driving me inside, but right at this moment, I am sitting here, feeling at peace.

There have been so many *kleine Schwierigkeiten* [little problems] and so much confusion over these past few days. But when I look at all the beauty around me, just waiting for me to find it, I know that none of the trials I'm going through will keep me from loving it here. I want so many things in life, and this is a big step for me. No matter what obstacles I might face here, I have to overcome them and persevere.

When the next six months glide into the sunset, I want to have gotten out of them all that I possibly could. I feel a compelling need to embrace the unknown that tantalizes and scares me at the same time, and live and breathe the newness around me in every way.

I don't want to be like others who have clung to our program and the American students, as a cushion on which to feel comfortable. This experience, for me, is about meeting at least a couple of German friends who will draw me into their lives and allow me to be a part of it. I want to understand their feelings, hopes, and dreams; how they see the world and their place in it.

Going up to people I don't know is not something I do very easily, but I also know that I can't just wait for others. To have the experience I want, I'll have to step out of what I've been familiar and comfortable with so far in life.

I hope, not necessarily for a boyfriend (which may be too time-consuming), but for at least one brief fling, to immerse myself into the culture here. And after the safety net of the program in Freiburg ends, I want to follow my own heart and go out on a limb, unafraid (or at least willing) to go it alone. That is why I plan to spend some time in Paris afterward. I want to prove to myself that I really can make it on my own, create an experience that is all mine – and work on my French.

It is time to stand on my own two feet and let my independence, which has never had the opportunity to blossom, show itself. I have lived a sheltered and protected life so far. Now, I'm shedding those comforts.

In a year and a few short months, I will graduate and be on my own. There is so much I suspect I could do – if I am strong and discover the inner fortitude that has not yet emerged in these first two decades of my life. I cannot conquer the world, but if I can conquer my fears, a mighty battle will be won.

It is time to put into practice everything I've learned so far. One thing I know is that I must radiate confidence, whether I have it yet or not. If I can even *seem* to have confidence, that will be enough to put into motion those first teetering steps, until I can develop it for real.

It is turning colder now, and I'm looking out across the mountains in the final moments before dusk. Everything I do seems to bring a new challenge, but I'm enjoying it anyway.

Someday, I may even look back on everything I'm going through and laugh. It all will have been so worth it.

The time is now – in these next six months in Europe – to make things happen. I only hope that I will make the right decisions and continue to follow my dreams.

Secrets from My Travel Diaries

➢ *Everything new comes with a little fear intermixed.*

➢ *Pushing through the fear is worth it – in exchange for what you gain.*

➢ *Radiate confidence to put in motion those first steps and build it as you go.*

CHAPTER 2

From Streaming to Cassettes

"Someday, I hope my diaries can be published. It is kind of a dream of mine to write a book so I can leave even a tiny mark on the world, made by the thoughts in my head." - 1997

Oct 7, 2021

Reading these pages now, it's hard to describe how it feels to read the words written in multi-colored ink. I feel like I'm stepping behind the veil of time. The movie reel of memory was weathered; now, it is back in full color. Details that were missing have been slotted back in. Images have come back into focus.

I'm traveling in reverse, skimming over the mountains and valleys in between. Smartphones have turned back to pay phones, streaming back to cassettes. I've crossed this bridge before with no GPS to guide me. Left to my own devices, the narrator of the story is me.

Waves of connected dots stream from my subconscious. *Clarity*. I'm going back to the simple truths before the complexities of life rolled in. The veil of years has shrouded the simple truths, but they haven't gone away.

It seems I knew exactly what I wanted then – at least for that time. I laid it all out with intention and set out to claim it.

"At 21, I'm embarking on a journey to figure out who I am...."

What did I figure out then? What pieces are missing now? It appears I've forgotten things I wish I'd remembered.

I keep going back to those words, *"Never again will you be this free."* It gives me chills to see how they shifted the angle of my lenses, and intermingled with the ink on those diaries. They cast a light outlined with a subtle heaviness. . . a shadow. . . a reminder that it was finite and fleeting. . .

Going overseas represented freedom – from the structure of school and the course that had been charted. Being there was my time to sail on adventures, to explore new waters, to splash paint on the opening canvas of adulthood. But on the other side of the bridge awaited a return to pressures and expectations.

And those pressures and expectations – both real and imagined – have been there ever since.

All at once, I see how *"Never again will you be this free"* has moved through the undercurrents in my life.

They still weigh upon me. . . The expectations I've worked tirelessly to meet. . . All the things I've done because I thought I should.

Those expectations are loosening their grip – but I have not broken free.

What was my answer then? I flip back and read:

"I cannot conquer the world, but if I can conquer my fears, a mighty battle will be won."

Fear. *Yes.* Fear of the unknown, fear of… I don't even know what. Just fear – but why? What am I afraid of?

It feels like nothing makes sense anymore.

Clarissa… She will understand. This time, I don't even bother to text her first to see if she's available. I just touch the home screen and hit the nearly-forgotten green "phone" icon.

She answers on the second ring.

"I was wondering when you would call," she says.

She gets it – just like she did then. We don't even need words.

We laugh – a little stiff at first. It's a shallow laughter that lingers in the throat, as if afraid to escape. Then, we start to let go. The laughter begins to deepen and crescendo, the sound waves intermingling through the phone.

The heaviness begins to break away. All at once, it's as if no time has passed since we were together in some distant land. . . In the middle of a dilemma that seemed like it had no way out – except that there was always a way.

There was always a way. . . because we were resourceful, and we knew what we wanted. And because we had each other, we could always just laugh.

At that moment, I feel free again – and full of fresh hope.

I think about those seminars when the facilitators ask, "If you could have a conversation with your younger self, what would you say?"

Perhaps, there's a twist. What if the question were reversed?

What if my 21-year-old self has something to teach me?

Could the mentor that I need be *me*?

I open up to where I left off and resume reading. . .

Secrets from My Travel Diaries

> ➤ *Life meanders – it's easy to lose yourself under the layers of who you think you "should" be.*

> ➤ *It's not too late to chart a new course.*

> ➤ *Everything you need is within you already – even if you can't see it.*

CHAPTER 3

Learning Everything Again

"I feel like there's so much that I don't know. Sometimes I can laugh it off without a problem, and other times I can't deal."

February 24, 1997

Tom lives in a different apartment complex, a bus ride away. This afternoon he went to his place to get some clothes for the next day, so he could stay over at Mike's. He ended up getting lost and returning about three hours later. Clarissa and I were so exhausted; we were about to go to bed when he finally got back. I guess I'm not the only one who struggles with directions. …

I woke up this morning feeling kind of crappy and only felt worse when I ate cereal with the German milk that tastes like cream (although it's supposed to be low fat). I don't understand the milk here in general, which comes in small boxes that don't need to be refrigerated until opened.

Over these past few days, I've been feeling run down. I've been sleeping well, but I never wake up completely rested. It's probably a combination of jet lag and the exhaustion from having to learn everything again.

Also, it's kind of weird being here while most other students (outside of those in my program) are on break. Most of the time I feel lost and alone in my apartment, and I try to avoid being there as much as possible. There's been no sign of my flatmate since that first day. Maybe she was just passing through on her way somewhere during the semester break.

The other day Clarissa and I were practicing German together, and she asked me how my night was. I responded matter-of-factly: *"Ich war ganz allein."* ["I was very alone."]. Someone walking behind us overheard what I said and started cracking up. (At least now I know that I can make people laugh in German, too.)

German immersion classes started today and go from nine o'clock to one-thirty in the afternoon, Monday through Thursday, for the next three weeks. Somehow, I tested into the highest level. Most of the students in my class have German parents and are very fluent. It's a bit intimidating at times, but all we've done so far is grammar, which is my strong suit, so I'm ahead of the game on that anyway.

It's kind of boring sitting in class for so long, but at least the professor is pretty laid back. We have two rather lengthy breaks, that officially are supposed to be only 15 minutes each, but the professor stretches them out for us.

After class, we went to the *Mensa* [cafeteria]. A lot of the other students from our program don't like it, but Clarissa, Anne, Mike, and Tom, and I think it is so incredibly good and cheap, at 17 deutsche marks for five meals [about $2 each]. Lunch at the *Mensa* is like a full-course meal, with soup, pasta and/or meat, and sometimes dessert. I think I'll actually miss it when it's closed over the weekend.

Errands seem to take forever here because we still aren't sure where we're going and what we should do. But I can tell already that a lot of the places that were unfamiliar a whole two days ago are now more familiar. I feel like I'm making less of a fool of myself about not knowing what to do, too.

With every day that passes, we find a few more cool places to go and cheaper places to buy food. And we become even more bonded to one another. I especially like Anne – aside from Clarissa, of course. Anne wants to go out a lot and meet Germans, so we share a common interest in that, among other things.

Sometimes I forget that I am in Germany because I am always with Americans, but we try to speak German a lot, so we can practice for when classes start. The other night, we were all sitting together in Clarissa's kitchen, eating German food, conversing in German, and listening to a German radio station. Could that be equivalent to a group of Germans in the U.S. speaking English, wearing cowboy hats, and dining on cheeseburgers? We had a good laugh about that.

Anyway… this afternoon, I went to a café with several others from class. The pastries in the window were so exquisite and enticing. We had so much fun looking at all the different kinds. Then we all ordered desserts and passed them so we could taste one another's.

I had some *Schokoladenkäsekuchen* [chocolate cheesecake], which was really good. Some of the fancier kinds must be an acquired taste, like the Black Forest Cake. Even though we're in the Black Forest of Germany, I realized I'm not a big fan of chocolate paired with cherry liqueur.

The only thing about the cafe we went to was that it was filled with older people, probably at least 60 years old. I guess we still have to find out where more of the student hangouts are. (Freiburg inhabitants are typically on both ranges of the spectrum: retirees who live here because it's the sunniest and warmest part of Germany, and students who attend university.)

It's been so busy with class and going out and getting to know people. Meanwhile, I still have the basic challenges (like having no pillow, sheets that fit the bed, or a phone that I can use to call the U.S.).

I tried to call my parents the other day and discovered with dismay that my phone still doesn't work. All I got when I dialed was some German lady on a recording. I ended up walking down the street to find a payphone in the middle of the night. It was so nice to talk with my parents, even though they feel so far away from the life I have here.

February 25, 1997

I feel like it's been difficult keeping up with all that's going on, but when I look at where I left off, I'm actually only two days behind. This time warp makes it seem like it's been so much longer.

After class yesterday, we had to go together as a group to fill out paperwork to register all over the city. It was really annoying and long (three hours), but Clarissa and I sat with Anne, Mike, and Tom, which was fun.

Mike and Tom had been out all night and were still a bit out of it. After filing all the paperwork, Tom turned to me and said with total seriousness, *"Wollt ihr mit Mike und mir schlafen?"* ["Do you want to sleep with Mike and me?"].

It turns out he meant *"einkaufen"* [go shopping] and was just spaced out. We had a laugh about that. I'm glad it was a misunderstanding. It's great having a couple of guys around who are totally fun without having to think about anything else.

It seems kind of strange to say, since I have only been here for a couple of weeks, but I'm already feeling like I don't want this time to end.

February 26, 1997

I am sitting outside the library, waiting for it to open at eight o'clock in the morning so that I can check my email before other people arrive. There are only a few computers, set up on high tables, so that you have to stand up the whole time. There's almost always a line.

It feels like I'm getting the hang of things here. I have a pillow now, and last night I finally did what I had been putting off: my laundry!

It took me a while to find the one random washing machine, which was locked in a tiny room on the fifth floor. Then, I had no idea how to use it, so I had to go into the kitchen on that floor and ask if anyone knew how. It was a bit embarrassing, but I did find someone to show me.

I managed to wash my clothes, and they seemed at least relatively clean. There was no dryer, so I hung them up all around my room on the clothesline I'd bought at *Kaufhof* [the local grocery store]. Then, I went to bed, surrounded by my wet clothes.

February 27, 1997

This afternoon, Clarissa, Anne, and I were riding the bus back from the city center to *Merzhauserstraße*. The bus stopped in front of it, but Anne got separated from us, couldn't open the door, and had to ride the bus until the next stop.

We watched her standing helplessly at the back of the bus as it drove further and further away. The look on Anne's face was so priceless that Clarissa and I couldn't help doubling over with laughter. When Anne returned about ten minutes later, she was mad at us for laughing about it. But then, after a few minutes, like with everything else, she was laughing along with us.

Tonight, we went over to Tom's apartment to cook dinner in his kitchen, which he shares with the other people in his wing of the apartment. There was stuff so crusted to the shelves it wouldn't come off: noodles that had been stuck to the coffee pot for an eternity and a pile of rusted silverware on the terrasse.

We had a hard time getting the stovetop to stay lit, so it took us forever to get the water to boil, but eventually, we did. Along with our spaghetti, we also tried to make garlic bread. However, there were only a few markings on the stove, as most of them had already worn off the dial. It turned out we must have chosen the wrong setting because the bread never got toasted.

We couldn't find enough utensils, either. Someone passing by happened to have some chopsticks in his room and went and got them for us.

To top off the meal, Mike and Tom had found some wine at the grocery store for only 3.79 deutsche marks [about $2] for two liters – dirt cheap but really good.

After the rather interesting meal that somehow turned out to be fun and edible, we laughed about everything that had taken place so far. I love the little group that the five of us created. When we're together, even cooking spaghetti in a sketchy pot on 100-year-old burners, and eating it with chopsticks, is so much fun.

February 28, 1997

I noticed this morning that a few things were different in the bathroom. Another one of my flatmates must have returned from break. I've been in and out a lot, though, and haven't seen anyone yet.

This afternoon Clarissa and I met up to go to *Kaufhof*. Some things, like finding laundry detergent that really works, still elude us. It's nice going together, though – even if neither one of us has any idea what to do.

Initially, I didn't expect that I would spend this much time with Clarissa on a day-to-day basis. I guess it's not so surprising it's turned out this way, though. We enjoy spending time with the same people and doing the same things. And I always know that I can truly depend on her, which means a lot.

The other night, Clarissa and I made dinner at my place. We got really confused by all the different trash cans in the kitchen. They all had different labels. After much discussion and second-guessing, we finally separated our trash into the bins.

A little while later, my housemate, Greta, came back. She headed directly into the kitchen, and I had a bad feeling when I heard her opening a trash bin. Sure enough, a few minutes later, I looked up to see her standing in the doorway, dangling a wrapper that we'd discarded.

I felt like a scolded child when she led us back into the kitchen and gave us a full explanation of all the trash receptacles and what types of trash go in each. My trash vocabulary in German is pretty limited, and I didn't catch the full explanation, so I'm a little nervous about getting it right (so much for creating a good impression).

Eating, in general, seems like it's always an adventure here. On Fridays, Mensa serves fish. I almost puked because they give you the whole fish, complete with eyes, head, and tail. I can't imagine eating something like that. It was a great relief when I realized I could order the vegetarian menu instead.

March 1, 1997

It's late afternoon, and I've been writing by the lake without a coat, with the sun shining over the mountains. I keep having to move benches because people keep sitting next to me.

A couple of people sat down and started lighting cigarettes, and blowing smoke in my face. On another bench, a grandmother sat down beside me, and her two grandchildren started shooting arrows from their bows at my feet.

Though moving benches has seemed so strange and a little annoying, I also know that nothing can stop me from loving it here. As I sit here, I feel like I'm in heaven.

This morning, Clarissa and I went for a hike, in pursuit of a well-known chapel and sanctuary dedicated to *Saint Odile,* in a suburb of Freiburg. The guide from our city tour recommended it, so we thought we'd check it out. (Apparently, Saint Odile was born blind, and her eyesight was miraculously restored when she was baptized. Now others make the pilgrimage to seek healing, too.)

We weren't sure exactly where it was, but there was a family walking by, and they told us where to go. Still not entirely clear about the directions, we turned off in the wrong direction and got turned around in the curved paths through the woods.

Next, we encountered a retired couple who were really nice and walked part of the way with us. They were charming people, and it was so much fun to practice our German with them. After a little while, they said they wanted to walk more slowly, though, and suggested we go on without them.

At that point, we were close enough to where there was signage to point the way. We followed the signs to the church with the spring water you're supposed to use to clean your eyes.

After checking out the area, we headed back, only to realize we weren't sure where "back" was because we had lost the signage. Then, we ran into a couple of students from the university. We ended up walking with them all the way to the middle of the city.

The entire way back, they told us all about the places around Freiburg that we should visit. Clarissa and I decided that it's a lot of fun not knowing where you're going: It's a great way to start a conversation!

I'm still completely amazed that I live here in Freiburg, Germany. More amazing still is that I'm starting to feel equipped to lead a normal life here, despite the occasional hiccup here and there.

I finally figured out what was going on with my laundry. Greta came with me to the laundry room and saw that I was using "washing machine cleaner" instead of "washing machine detergent." (I was wondering why it said, "Protection for your washing machine" on the back of the bottle.)

I had to get another washing machine card, which is really a pain because you can only buy them between eight and nine o'clock in the evening on Mondays and Wednesdays. The instructions said to put the card into the machine again after washing your clothes, but I pushed the wrong button and ended up buying another wash instead. (Fortunately, Mike was walking by, and he quickly gathered up some laundry and used it.)

Then, I put too many clothes on the clothesline, and it started to fall. I grabbed for the clothesline, knocking over the cactus I'd bought to spruce up my stark, white room. The cactus fell onto the floor and got dirt everywhere, but I think I managed to salvage it.

It's humbling – but necessary – to ask for help with just about everything I try to do. At least now I'm meeting people I can ask.

March 2, 1997

I am breaking the ice with Greta a little more every day. My recent breakthrough started with another mishap. We were running out of food for dinner because we always forget how long it is from Friday until Monday when we can shop again. (All the grocery stores close Saturdays at six o'clock in the evening here and don't open again until Monday.)

We ended up with very little food between us on Sunday, so we made a meager dinner, pooling together all the food we had.

When I got back to my apartment, I told Greta about forgetting the stores were closed. She said, "Very different from the 24-hour markets in your country, isn't it?" Then, she said that she'd forgotten about the limited hours before, too, and had done the same thing!

Secrets from My Travel Diaries

> ➢ *Live overseas at least once, so that you can approach life with childlike wonder – and gain a new perspective on what you thought you knew.*

> ➢ *Ask for help – it not only makes life much easier, but it also makes strangers into friends.*

CHAPTER 4

The Dating Scene

"I just don't understand the rules of the game here."

March 4, 1997

The dating scene here really mystifies me. I see couples all around. However, I'm pretty sketchy about how you go from meeting a guy, to getting locked in a passionate embrace, like the couple I saw the other day at the library.

Tonight we met a big group of Americans – maybe 20 or so – to celebrate someone's 21st birthday. The fun thing about being at the bar was that several of us started plotting ways to meet German men.

Some people who were "in the know" said that most of the German men they've met are shy and don't come up to you. However, if you come up to them, they'll hang out with you for hours and give you their phone number and tell you that they want to see you again.

I'm trying to take to heart the H. Jackson Brown Jr. quote that Stephanie gave me, *"Twenty years from now, you will be more disappointed by the things you didn't do than by the ones you did."* So, I've decided that if I have to make the first move here, that's what I'm going to do.

One thing I noticed was that the guys in our program seem to have no idea how things work here, either. As the night continued, a few of them tried to dance with German women, who looked at them completely appalled. (It seems that no one comes up to you or dances with you randomly at clubs like they do in the U.S. The only exception seemed to be one very drunk guy, but he was really just flailing around.)

Anne has started calling the German way of meeting people a *neues Spiel* [new game]. I guess that's what it is: a new game with new rules. It seems, we have no idea how the game is played.

March 7, 1997

Tonight, Clarissa, Anne, and I were hanging out at one of the bars drinking *dunkles Bier* [German dark beer]. We immediately noticed two good-looking guys sitting at a nearby table and began to make eye contact with them from across the room.

Anne dared me to go over and talk to them, and this new, courageous me actually did. I walked over to them as casually as I could, but when I got there, I realized I didn't know what to say. So I just paused by their table, looked over and said, *"Wie geht's?"* ["How are you doing?"]

From there, we just started talking. Then, I told them I had *"ein paar Freundinnen"* [a couple of friends] with me, and they told me to bring them over.

The guys' names were Fritz and Otto. Both of them were already out of school and working in the business world. Fritz lived in Freiburg but told me he spent two months traveling from coast to coast in the U.S. for vacation. Also, he said that he'd been to Cincinnati, Ohio, visiting a branch of the shipping company where he works (small world!).

Otto was visiting Fritz from Heidelberg. He spoke a very different dialect that I didn't understand. Though he was good about speaking *Hochdeutsch* [standard German] to me, I still couldn't understand him nearly as well as I could Fritz.

After a little while, Fritz and Otto invited us to go with them to another bar down the street. They stayed for another round of drinks. Then they had to leave because they were catching a bus to go skiing in Switzerland at four-thirty in the morning.

Before they left, Fritz gave me his business card and made a point of telling me that he was looking forward to my call. I asked him if it was okay that I had come up and randomly talked to them. Fritz smiled and said that was *"kein Problem"* ["no problem"] in this cute way.

March 10, 1997

The evening with Fritz has been playing in my mind, off and on, for the past few days. It's really not that big of a deal, but somehow, to me, it is. I don't want to read too much into things.

It's amazing to me that he would even have any interest in me. I feel so incredibly different from the German women I've met, but at the same time, not that different. It's kind of difficult to explain.

I keep thinking about how he gave me his card and told me to call him, as if he felt the same vibes. Of course, maybe he does that often, with lots of people.

Somehow, I can't help but feel completely fascinated with every aspect of him. Still, I'm trying to stay guarded because I have no idea what he really intends – if anything.

This afternoon, I was hanging out with a couple of people from my program, and they convinced me that it was time to find out what was going on. So, I decided to ring Fritz's number when I got back to my apartment (after all the trouble making international calls, local ones are super easy!).

Someone, who I guess was his housemate, answered. He said he had "no idea" where Fritz was but could take a message. I felt kind of awkward leaving a message and was close to just hanging up. But then I thought better of it and decided to just go for it.

After all, if he's forgotten who I am or if he didn't really want me to call him, he could just not call back. (For all I know, he could already have a girlfriend. I hope not, but I have no idea how things work here.)

This evening, I went out with a couple of people from the program. When I got back to my apartment, I was in the bathroom getting ready for bed when the phone rang. I thought at first it must be for one of my flatmates. But when I answered the phone, a deep German male's voice came through the phone – asking for me (!).

Fritz and I talked for 20 or 30 minutes. I enjoyed our conversation tremendously. It's so unbelievable to me how well I can talk to and understand him, even though he never speaks any English. (He says that he finds English difficult and would prefer that we talk in German.)

We talked about all kinds of things. I told him about my grammar class, how it is so long and goes on for hours each day, but that it's helping me improve my German. To that, he replied that my German was already good!

When he said that, I felt kind of shy and told him I'd gotten a lot better but still didn't *sound* German. To that, he said: *"Nein, aber es klingelt sehr gut."* [No, but it sounds really good.]

At the end of the conversation, *he asked if he could see me again.*

The whole conversation made me so excited that I couldn't fall asleep for a long time.

Since then, thoughts of Fritz keep playing in my mind. *Am I reading too much into things? Is he really interested in me?* I'm just amazed how we could talk for so long on the phone, completely in German, and we seemed to click just as I would have if he were a guy I'd met at home.

It all seems so random how we met and then had this great phone conversation. I'm feeling this incredible fascination with him. Does he feel the same for me? I guess maybe he does; otherwise, he wouldn't have given me his card or called me back in the first place.

Maybe he'll never call again, though.

It could be that I dreamed this whole thing up, and it's just an illusion.

Maybe he's really not who I think he is. It's so hard to tell.

All I know is I want to know more about what makes him tick. I want to know everything about him.

After only talking with him twice, I am ready to sail away on a whim. My reservations (and wondering whether he already has a girlfriend) are the only anchor that is keeping my feet on the ground.

I still have no idea how to date here. Yet, I'm shining with the light of fascination, and my heart is ready to soar to the clouds.

March 12, 1997

I feel like I am doing so much more work than I should be, trying to get ahold of Fritz. He might feel the same, though, because I am not home very often, either. Without an answering machine, it's difficult to ever get in touch with each other.

Despite the thoughts of Fritz darting through my mind, I managed to focus enough to tackle the six-page practice test to pass my German immersion class. After getting it just about finished, I got really sick of it and needed a break, so I decided to call Fritz again.

This time when I called, he was home (!). We talked for an hour, not about anything much – just got to know each other, covering all kinds of topics.

During our conversation, there would be certain words that I wouldn't know. I would look them up in my German dictionary, but I didn't always know how to pronounce them. The way I'd say them would sound funny to him, and he would chuckle in this really cute way and say, *"Sag es noch einmal. Das klingelt so gut."* [Say it again. It sounds so good.]

I still just don't know what he expects out of this. As much as I enjoyed the conversation, a little of the elation from our initial meeting has worn off, which is good. I don't want to get my hopes up over someone I just met, although he does seem so awesome.

No matter what happens (as I fall into bed), I can't help feeling a sense of wonder about how much I love it here.

March 14, 1997

I am feeling homesick and totally deflated.

Fritz called and asked me to hang out with him and his friends. At first, I told him I wasn't sure I'd be able to make it. His invitation conflicted with the "meet-the-professors" party with our program, in preparation for the start of the semester. (My course schedule will consist of classes through our program with other Americans, and classes at the university with German students.)

The meet-the-professors party was a must-attend event, but I was torn about missing the chance to meet up with Fritz again. When I got back after the party, I decided to call him. He wasn't there, of course, so I talked to his flatmate again. He encouraged me to meet them at the movie theater and instructed me where to go.

I debated over and over whether I should go or not. The thought of going by myself was nerve-racking. I wasn't sure about meeting his friends or what I'd do if he actually had a girlfriend.

Mike and I hung out in the kitchen, going over every angle of the decision and sorting through all the conflicting thoughts in my head. Finally, he gave me some very simple advice, "If it's important to you, go. *Wenn es dir egal ist* [If it doesn't matter to you], just forget it."

That did it for me. It definitely *did* matter to me. And I had to know where this was leading – if anywhere. If, within his group of friends, I could see a girlfriend, then at least I'd know before getting in too deep.

It was only about 10 minutes before the movie was supposed to start when I took off for the bus. I caught it just as it was coming down the street in front of *Merzhauserstraße.*

When I got to the movie theater, it was dark, and the movie had already started, so I found a seat in the back and met up with them afterward. (It was no big deal sitting by myself and watching the movie – it seems like it is quite normal in Germany. It's funny how things I would never do in the U.S. seem like no big deal here.)

When I met up with Fritz and his friends, I immediately saw that the group included a few couples, a small group of guys – and his girlfriend. The two of them weren't holding hands or anything, but I could tell it was her. She is tall, blonde, pretty, and seems very nice. I couldn't help but feel devastated, but I managed to stick it out and had a decent time anyway.

After the movie, we went to play a trivia game at an Irish pub. I knew several of the answers others didn't know, which made for some good conversation. The whole time, I traded off talking with people, including Fritz's roommate, who showed up after I did.

I feel so homesick right now because I just can't understand how things work here.

Deep down, I already suspected that he had a girlfriend. Somehow it was implied, though he never said anything specifically. Still, it felt like there was something between us, beyond friendship.

The "rational me" realizes that Fritz did nothing wrong. He never led me on – he was just incredibly interesting and fun. It's still so hard to understand what happened, though. If a guy in the U.S. did something like that, his girlfriend would *definitely* be jealous.

There was no sign of jealousy from her, though. Here, it seems perfectly normal and accepted for someone like Fritz to want to get to know someone like me, just for the sake of it, with no other expectations.

Maybe in this culture, people have mastered the art of having friends of the opposite sex and dealing with it in a mature fashion – even if they have a boyfriend or girlfriend. For some reason, I never learned how to do that, with the exception of Mike and Tom.

It is overwhelming to feel tossed into a country where I have to start all over again and play by different rules.

March 15, 1997

I've been thinking a lot about whether I'll ever call Fritz again.

At first, I thought I wouldn't. Now I'm thinking, maybe I will.

By never calling him again, I've realized I would be showing him that he means more to me than I want to let on. We had such good conversations; I'd rather be his friend than nothing at all. And I'm here in Freiburg to meet Germans, so I don't want to cut off German ties.

I'm so disappointed because we seemed to get along so well, and I so enjoyed our conversations.

Admittedly, we only had a few conversations, though.

And honestly, I really don't know him very well.

What I do know is a little more about what the man on the plane coming over here meant when he talked about the language and the cultural differences. They *can* make it seem as though you're looking through a glazed window. Perhaps the whole thing with Fritz seemed far rosier than it ever really was. It definitely made the whole thing into something it's not.

Is it just as well? Would this whole thing have led to an "international boo-boo" at some point? I have absolutely no idea.

Even if I still feel a little disappointed, I'll get over it. I love that getting to know Fritz has helped me understand the perspective of someone who grew up in a different life, an entire ocean away from me. Just knowing him has been a great experience, even if we can't be more than friends.

In a lot of ways, this is an opportunity. I was blind to anyone else when I thought there could be something with Fritz, but now I am free. There are, after all, so many other people here to meet and get to know.

Ultimately, I still haven't figured out the rules of this game. But I do know the game *I'm* playing. And that is to learn everything I can and have a great time – which is far more important than any crush.

Secrets From My Travel Diaries

➢ *Have the courage to go out and figure out how a new game is played.*

➢ *Even if you lose, you win when you decide what game you want to play.*

CHAPTER 5

Burning the Candle at Both Ends

"I'm taking every opportunity – with no regrets."

March 16, 1997

Some of the American students told me their German flatmates have been hard to get to know. I've found that true in some ways, but I've also noticed that with most people if you are willing to make the first move, you don't have to do much else.

That, at least, is how it was with Clarissa's flatmates, Hilda and Mark. For a little while, they seemed really closed. They didn't even say hello.

Then, one day Mike, Tom, Clarissa, Anne, and I were all hanging out together. (Somehow, Tom finagled a move from his former apartment to one that is two doors down from Mike, so we are all together in the same apartment complex now.)

Anyway, I got up the courage to go up and talk with Hilda and Mark, who were sitting at the kitchen table. Well, it turns out they're really nice! I asked them to go to the disco with us, but they said, "Another time."

Still, it was a step.

The next night Clarissa greeted me with the news that Hilda and Mark were hanging out with Mike and Tom and wanted to go to the disco with us. And, apparently, they made a point of asking Clarissa if I was coming because they found me "*ganz lustig*" [very funny].

A small battle toward acceptance had been won!

We joined in the drinking games for a while, all of us sitting around the kitchen table, speaking a mixture of English and German. Then, Clarissa, Anne, and I wanted to catch the last bus and went to get ready. (The last bus comes by at ten o'clock at night. After that, the *Nachtbus* [night bus] schedule kicks in, which is less frequent and costs twice as much – 7 deutsche marks [about $4].)

When we got back, Mike, Tom, Hilda, and Mark were still wrapped up in their game. Finally, we got everyone out the door just as the bus turned the corner. All seven of us, five Americans and two Germans, streamed haphazardly out on *Merzhauserstraße* and ran toward the bus.

We made it just before the bus pulled away. Our laughter filled the silence in the near-empty bus, all the way to the city center.

The club we went to had one big room and multiple small ones. There was a "techno room" with weird lights that Anne loved. Most of the songs were in English, intermixed with songs in German and French.

Hilda saw us singing along to one of the songs in English and rolled her eyes, saying it must be "so boring" to understand every word in the song. We totally cracked up because she looked so funny, exaggerating the mouth movements in English with her thick German accent. She had never spoken to us in English before – so much fun!

Later on, Clarissa, Mike, and I got separated from the others on the way to another club. We decided to head back to *Merzhauserstraße* but realized we had no idea where it was. After walking for a long time up some mountain road lined with mansions, we found a phone and called a taxi, only to find out that we'd been only a few minutes' drive away.

Exhausted, I fell asleep in the front hallway on the couch in Clarissa's apartment suite. I woke up cold and uncomfortable, found a blanket, and moved to the couch next to the kitchen table.

The next day we had an optional trip to the *Schwarzwald* [Black Forest] with our program and were supposed to meet everyone at nine-fifteen in the morning. I was startled when Clarissa woke me from a sound sleep after running around the apartment, looking for me everywhere.

She disappeared to knock on Anne's upstairs door to ask her if she wanted to go. A few minutes later, they both appeared in front of me in their PJs, asking if I thought we should go. The whole thing felt surreal; I was so groggy.

Finally, we decided to go for it. By then, we only had five minutes to get to the bus. In some ways, we would have been better off skipping that trip. It was tough getting through the day, but it would probably have been better if we hadn't been absolutely exhausted.

One of the most painful hours was touring a museum filled with antiques. It was conducted by an older gentleman with a dialect I could barely understand, who greeted us as if he hadn't had a visitor in decades. I thought his explanations would never end.

Touring the city, we saw a big group of elementary school kids. It struck me that it's kind of like I'm back to their age again, with my German language abilities. In truth, though, I'm nowhere near their level yet. Still, I bet I could give them a run for their money when it comes to grammar, as it's been pounded into my head daily.

At the end of the day, we stopped at a café and had coffee and rum cakes. On the bus back to Freiburg, our professor gave a brief lecture and then played some German folk songs. (At least the coffee woke me up a little.)

I guess every day here feels like at least a week because of all the new experiences and ideas that I'm exposed to daily. My mind is swirling with German folk songs, coffee, rum cake, and what I could piece together about the docent's antiques.

Aside from classes, we've been hanging out with Hilda and Mark (who we affectionately started calling our *"Mitbewohner"* [flatmates], pretty much every day. Last night we went out dancing, followed by another exhausting day of class. Tom missed class because he and Mike had stayed up until seven o'clock in the morning with the *Mitbewohner*. He slept until four-thirty in the afternoon that day, but somehow Mike managed to go to class and stay up the whole time.

Last night, Hilda and Mark weren't around, and Clarissa, Anne, Mike, Tom, and I had dinner together on our own. Tom made homemade potatoes from a huge bag he bought for 89 *pfennige* ($0.50). We also had *wurst* [sausage] and *knödel* [dumplings]. I think that was the best dinner we have had in Germany so far.

After dinner, we took the bus to a bar in the middle of the city, catching the last one back before the *Nachtbus*. When we got back to Clarissa and Mike's apartment, we found Mark sitting alone at the kitchen table, playing chess with a pocket computer. It was the first time I'd seen him without Hilda, and it felt strange to see him there alone.

I guess everything we'd been doing had caught up with Hilda, too. Mark said she was exhausted and had gone to bed at nine o'clock. I totally understand where Hilda is coming from. It seems that because I'm young, I should be able to handle anything, but unfortunately, even youth has its limits. Somehow, Mike and Tom outlast us every night, no matter how late we stay up.

Mike and Tom get on each other's nerves a lot. They don't really get along, but they always seem to be together. They do the funniest things.

One day, we all went to *Deutsche Bank* to set up our bank accounts. When it was their turn in line, they said, *"Wir sind Ausländer, und wir möchten ein Konto eröffnen."* [We're foreigners, and we'd like to open a bank account."] It was a funny introduction, but I guess it worked because we were able to set up our accounts, all in German.

It's great having these kinds of friends. No matter what we're doing, we always have a great time as long as we're together.

I haven't had much time to even think about home. But one day after class, Clarissa and I met Melissa, a classmate from our school in Ohio who is studying in Heidelberg and was passing through Freiburg on the way to Switzerland. We sat outdoors, had *Eiskaffee* [iced coffee], and talked about what was happening at school.

I feel so incredibly far away from there because I haven't had a stitch of news since I got here. It feels like Ohio is another world, and I have no idea what is happening there. Being here, it's like my world is expanding in a whole new way. I'm meeting people from all over the world like never before.

The other day, Greta had a friend over from South America named Maria. Maria didn't speak German that well and interjected all kinds of random Spanish words into her sentences. This made her difficult to understand (but also made me want to learn Spanish).

Clarissa and Anne were coming over to do homework and then check out a bar I'd heard about from someone in my German grammar class. I decided to ask Greta and Maria if they wanted to go along, and they did. It was the best time.

So much has been going on lately that I'd stopped thinking so much about Fritz, who I thought I hadn't heard from. Today Greta asked me about him, though, and told me that he's called at least five times, always when I'm not home.

He never leaves a message and seems to talk with different people each time. Greta didn't even realize it until Felix said, "Some guy who spoke perfect German keeps calling Stacey."

That cracked me up, how Felix said that. Could he not imagine that a real, live German might actually call me? It was so funny.

I know now that nothing will come of Fritz and me, but already it's not that big of a deal. At last, I've reached the point of being okay with just being friends with him. I know that, eventually, I will meet the right man. For now, though, I am content not to get too serious about anything.

It's still hard to understand how his girlfriend would not be jealous of how he flirted with me, called me all those times, and even keeps calling me now. Is it that she doesn't know, or are they far more understanding about this sort of thing in German culture?

Either way, I'm going to do the mature thing: Act as if I never hoped anything would go on between us and just be his friend. It's time to move on, anyway. We have lots of fun trips coming up and exciting times ahead.

We have holidays and breaks throughout the semester, and we're planning to go a different direction every time. It will be a whirlwind of going to class, exploring Europe, returning to Freiburg, and doing it all again.

When the train leaves the station, I want to be on it...

Secrets from My Travel Diaries

> ➢ *Create your vision and take steps toward it every day.*

> ➢ *The passage of time puts things into perspective.*

> ➢ *Enjoy the little things along the way.*

CHAPTER 6

French with a Side of German (Strasbourg & Paris)

"It was exhilarating to be in France, speaking in French and German and translating for my friends."

March 14, 1997

We had to meet at eight-thirty in the morning to go on our program trip to Strasbourg in Alsace, France. Making the trip was easier than last time, because we got to bed at two o'clock in the morning.

I was incredibly excited about the trip because I'd wanted to go to Strasbourg since I studied about it in high school. It's hard even to imagine how you can drive merely one hour and be in another country where everyone speaks another language. It excited me to no end to hear everyone speaking French.

During our free time after our city tour, we bought some postcards and asked the shopkeeper where to get a reasonably inexpensive, authentic French meal. She recommended a place offering a nice sit-down lunch for only $6.50. I ordered *Quiche Lorraine* (very appropriate, since we were in *Alsace-Lorraine*), followed by a *petit pan au chocolat*, which is also typical of the region.

I got to speak with the waitress in French. Tom said he thought it was the coolest thing that I speak French and that he couldn't wait for our upcoming trip to Paris.

After lunch, we went to *"Le Haut-Koenigsbourg"* castle, then to a winery on the way back. The winemaker, who was hilarious and sometimes perverted, gave the tour in German. Sometimes he forgot, though, and started going off in French. We tasted four different kinds of white wine. As he served them, he kept repeating over and over that, *"A meal without wine is like a day without sun."*

Speaking French had confused my brain, and my words were coming out in a mixed jumble of French and German. After that trip, though, I started to get the two languages sorted and felt confident enough to start making the phone calls for our trip planning. (Our German immersion is about to conclude, then we have a break before the start of the semester and another week off for Easter.)

Clarissa had been trying to connect with a Belgian exchange student named Jules to see if we could visit him in Brussels. I tried calling his house, but he wasn't around, so I talked with his dad. Only German came out of my mouth at first, but I managed to get back on track and get my point across in French. Then, I called to reserve Easter weekend in Nice on the French Riviera.

Clarissa, Anne, and I went to reserve our seats on the train for our upcoming trips. (On our first week off, between German immersion and the start of the semester, we're going to Paris, Brussels, and Amsterdam. On Easter week, we decided to go to Barcelona, the French Riviera, and Italy.)

We asked about reservations at the first travel agency we went to, and the ticket prices seemed very expensive. Finally, after minor confusion, we realized they only sold plane tickets there.

At the next travel agency, the guy took one look at our itinerary and said, *"Diese Leute wollen ganz Europa sehen. Ich brauche eine Pause."* [These people want to visit the entire continent of Europe. I need a break.] So, we were referred to his colleague, a kind and patient older gentleman in a bowtie named Hans.

We ended up staying at the *Reisebüro* [tourist agency] with Hans for two hours. That was how long it took to turn our itinerary, carefully crafted to maximize the 24 hours of travel, into a booked reservation. There was a problem with the computer that made everything go super slow. Also, we ran into a glitch about the time our train was leaving. Somehow, the computer system was counting two days against our Eurail passes instead of one.

Hans was super patient working through everything, but I couldn't believe it could possibly take that long. We ended up spending most of the beautiful day inside, but there wasn't much we could do. Everyone has the same spring break over Easter, so we definitely needed to book those reservations.

Our shopping trip with Mike and Tom got delayed because of all the computer trouble, but they didn't seem to mind. In fact, the funny thing was that they waited with us pretty much the entire time. They left a couple of times briefly, but mostly they just sat there with us, keeping us entertained while the computer chugged along.

I can't even imagine having the patience to do what Mike and Tom did. They always seem so carefree and act like they have all the time in the world. It's nice to be around people like that because I always try to pack in too much and end up stressed out.

When we finally had everything worked out with our reservations, the five of us went to *Kaufhof* to get smaller shampoos for our trip. (We will be living out of our travel backpacks and don't want them to be too heavy.) We took the elevator upstairs and ended up getting turned around in another part of the store that was off on its own. Finally, we went outside and back in again and managed to find the shampoos.

The next thing we had to do was find the place that sold hostel cards. I couldn't make reservations at the hostel in Paris because we didn't have the card. The only other alternative that was within our budget was a hostel run by nuns. It didn't require a card, but had a curfew of ten-thirty at night. We had a lot of trouble finding the place to buy the cards and almost had to call the nuns, but we finally found it just as we were about to give up.

We spent a lot of time pouring over *The Lonely Planet* so that we could figure out what we wanted to do and plan out how much money to exchange for each country we'd be visiting. We went to the bank to change the currencies, putting each set into a separate envelope for each country we were visiting. (Our economics professor gave a lecture about the euro, which will be rolled out in a few years. For now, each country has its own individual currency.)

I feel a little nervous about all the money we are spending on traveling and going out. Although we are not being excessive, we will definitely end up spending a lot of money. I told Dad about being worried about it. He said that was why I'd earned the money in the first place, so I should just enjoy my adventure.

When I checked my email at the library, I'd gotten an email back from John, a friend of my dad, who moved to Paris years ago, got married, got divorced, and ended up staying there. He confirmed that he can meet me in Paris while we're there and asked if I could bring a *curriculum vitae* (the French version of a resume), so he can help me get a job when I go to Paris after the semester ends.

I didn't have a CV prepared, so I started drafting one right away. Going back and forth from the program office to make updates on the computer was a pain, so I thought I'd find someone to look at it first. I saw one of the French exchange students, Amelie, walking into my apartment complex, went right up to her, and asked for help. She was super nice and helped me proofread it.

Finding the right accents on the German keyboard at the program office was frustrating. The keys were all in different places. A French guy, who I found quite good-looking, helped me proofread what I'd written. Afterward, we got into a conversation about a trip he'd made to the U.S. (It seems like everyone around here has been there.)

I read over my resume back at my apartment, found a typo, and had to go all the way back to the office again. Luckily, I found another French student available to look it over again.

After having been through three French students, I really hope my CV is finally right. I'm out of time now. Tomorrow morning, we are boarding the train to Paris.

March 17, 1997

Clarissa, Anne, and I left our apartment and took the bus to the train station. We ended up having to ditch Mike and Tom because when we stopped by to pick them up to walk to the bus stop, they weren't even packed. They were mad about spending the extra money on a taxi, but they did beat us to the train.

We had a few problems once we got off the train to Basel, Switzerland because we had gotten off at the wrong stop and had to take a taxi to a different station. Since we hadn't expected to stop in Switzerland, we had no Swiss money. Luckily, the taxi driver took deutsche marks. I had to sit on Anne's lap so that we could all fit in one cab, but we made it to the right station.

Somehow, we managed to catch our connecting train to Paris. I have no idea how we will know when to get off when we get there. They don't announce anything, and there are multiple train stations.

March 18, 1997

It was a long, uncomfortable night trying to sleep, sitting up on the train. At one point, we all woke up at the same time because our legs had fallen asleep.

We arrived in Paris at seven o'clock this morning, and Mike and Tom's friends, Susan and Tammy, came to meet us when we got off the train. (They were both studying in Paris and seemed to know everything that was going on – and how to get there.)

We dropped our stuff off at the hostel and went on a whirlwind tour, starting at Cemetery *Pere Lachaise*. At Jim Morrison's grave, Mike and Tom brought beer to drink on it, which I guess is some long-standing tradition. An armed guard appeared out of nowhere, snatched their beers, and poured them out.

After visiting Oscar Wilde's grave, we headed to *Sacre Coeur*. Being there made me catch my breath, like it did when I was 16, and visited it for the first time. However, the effect was a little more muted – not quite the same.

When I was 16, Paris was the first city outside of the U.S. and Canada I'd ever visited. I was so starstruck and mesmerized by everything I saw then. It's as if it's not even the same city now.
Albeit with its own unique charm, Paris looks a lot more like the other cities I've visited than I expected. I guess it's really me that has changed, I've been to more places since then, and I'm much more independent now.

Speaking French again was fun. I kept getting confused, though, because we decided to continue speaking German to one another to keep up the practice. One time Clarissa and I were sitting together on the metro, speaking German. I heard someone on the other side of me speaking French, and something switched in my head. I flipped to French in mid-sentence, and Clarissa got a look on her face like I was nuts. I had no idea why.

By the time we left *Sacre Coeur*, I felt about to collapse. It was already nearly three o'clock in the afternoon, and we'd barely eaten or slept. Clarissa and I defected from the tour of the Dali Museum and got a *crepe au miel* [crepe with honey] on the street instead. Finally, we all stopped for a lunch of quiche and fries.

With renewed energy, we went to the catacombs, a limestone passageway filled with bones and skulls arranged in rather interesting ways. There were all kinds of sayings carved into the stone in the walls, all pertaining to death in one way or another. (I guess a couple of the cemeteries were not dug deep enough, and the bones kept resurfacing and causing health hazards. Someone had the brainy idea to move all the bones down to the catacombs, so that's what they did.)

After the catacombs, we went to an Italian restaurant for happy hour. We had some beer mixed with tequila, kind of like a *Radler* in Germany. Then, we went to the *Centre Pompidou* and to *Les Halles* to enjoy a beautiful view of the city at night.

It was kind of weird not hanging out with Mike and Tom as much. The whole day, they mostly talked to Susan and Tammy, with Clarissa, Anne, and me trailing behind. The whirlwind tour was pretty efficient, though, and not having to worry about directions was really nice.

After *Les Halles,* Clarissa, Anne, and I went off on our own for a while and were supposed to meet up with the four of them for dinner later. We were so tired that we missed our stop and ended up riding the metro all the way to the end of the line. We didn't even figure it out until the metro stopped, and just sat there without moving.

We had to exit and go through the turnstiles again, only to find that our tickets were no longer valid. This incredibly nice older gentleman behind us scanned his pass for us, and we were able to get back to our stop.

When we finally got to the fountain where we were supposed to meet, Mike, Tom, Susan, and Tammy were nowhere to be found. After looking around for them for a while, we finally left to find a restaurant on our own. The street was lined with places, with people calling out from every restaurant, trying to drum up business. It felt a bit pushy.

Finally, we selected a place and were deep in conversation when I saw a rat crawling across the wall. I let out a cry. The waitress kept saying it was no big deal, but we had other opinions. We paid as quickly as possible and made a hasty exit, practically rolling on the floor laughing.

It took us a while to find our metro again, but we made it back to the hostel with no problems after that. (Back at the hostel, we exchanged stories with Mike and Tom. They told us they'd waited over half an hour and finally selected a nearby restaurant where they could keep a lookout for us, but we never saw each other.)

March 19, 1997

Here we are at our hostel, catching up on our diaries and waiting for Mike and Tom. We set our alarm so that we could shower, because the hot water goes away at eight o'clock in the morning. Breakfast ends at nine-fifteen, and lock-out starts at ten o'clock in the morning, so Mike and Tom had better hurry up.

Susan and Tammy couldn't meet us until this afternoon, so the five of us went for a walk on the Seine in the morning. We tried to find the *Jardin de Tuileries* but looked at the map wrong and never ended up finding it.

By that time, Mike and Tom's friends had arrived with another huge list of places for us to visit. It's funny that Mike and Tom have friends like these. I would think they'd prefer to spend their vacation sitting at a pub rather than running around from one tourist attraction to another.

Our first stop on the tour was the *Arc de Triomphe,* one of my favorite attractions in Paris. Clarissa, Anne, and I lingered up there for a while – too long, I guess. By the time we got back down, we had somehow managed to lose the group again.

As it turned out, though, we enjoyed hanging out and sightseeing by ourselves. It had gotten a little old being led around without much choice about what to do. We went to the *Champs-Elysées,* which was absolutely spilling over with people. And this time, we found the *Jardin de Tuileries.* The whole garden was already in bloom and incredibly beautiful.

The only lunch we'd had was a *croissant au jambon* [croissant with ham] we'd grabbed on the way to the *Arc de Triomphe.* By six-thirty in the evening, we were absolutely starved. However, most restaurants don't open until seven o'clock in Paris, as nightlife starts pretty late.

There was a restaurant that served Indian cuisine, which Clarissa and I had never tried before, but that Anne (who is from Los Angeles) absolutely loved. We walked in, seeing that the door was open, but the waiter said we had to come back at seven o'clock.

For the entire 20-minute wait, we sat on a park bench, talking about how hungry we were. Finally, it was seven o'clock, and we could go back in. Ironically, this time the doors were closed, but the restaurant was open.

The restaurant was small and seemed authentic. We drank *lassi* (a yogurt drink) and had *naan* (bread), basmati rice, and curry vegetables. For dessert, we had *halwa,* a spongy thing that looked like Colby cheese but tasted wonderful. The *lassi* was amazingly good with the spicy food, and it completely soothed the taste of it.

It was truly a delicious meal. We dropped around $17 U.S. for it, but it was well worth it. We rarely go out for dinner in Freiburg and typically only spend about $25 U.S. per week on food, so I think we can occasionally afford to splurge.

After dinner, we went back to our hostel and drank wine in the kitchen area where we ate breakfast. We met some other travelers hanging out there, too, and they told us about their travels.

March 21, 1997

We were excited when we saw the German-French dictionary sitting on top of our roommate's suitcase in our four-person room. We've been gone so much, though, that we were never able to catch her. (When we went to bed, she was already snoring – in the loudest and strangest way I've ever heard. Fortunately, we were too tired to notice for long.)

This morning, Clarissa opened her eyes to see the roommate cleaning her crotch in the middle of the room! After we were all dressed and ready for the day, we chatted with her as she perched on the edge of her bed, a beret cocked on the side of her head.

She told us that she was 40 years old and had been traveling for the past year. Right in the middle of the conversation, she whipped out an instrument consisting of about five pipes stuck together, blew out a couple of scales, and put it away. The conversation didn't go very far after that.

After breakfast, I caught the metro by myself to meet John. I ended up accidentally getting off at the wrong stop and found myself standing in front of the *SNCF* [France's state-owned railway company]. This French guy in a uniform said that I had committed a violation by being there and that I had to pay a fine of 100 francs [about $17].

I tried to reason with him because I had no clue what was going on, but I got so flustered and upset that I could barely talk. He told me I had to remember to breathe and would not budge from his stance.

Finally, after about 10 minutes, I extracted a bill from my money belt, handed it to him, and got out of there as fast as I could. I guess the bright side was that I didn't have any trouble understanding his French.

It took me a while to compose myself, but fortunately, I had been running early to the interview. When I finally got there, I went into the interview much stronger, fired up with telling myself how that guy could kiss my American ass.

John and I spent about two hours together, with him testing my French and asking me questions about what kind of position I was looking for. He is even going to let me use his apartment in Paris this summer because he will be on vacation in the south of France.

At the end of our meeting, he took my CV and offered to make some connections for me. The economy is tough, with unemployment at about 12% in France. However, he said that I have a chance at a temporary position because I have a *piston* [connection], which he said is the only way anyone gets a job in France.

After the interview, I had arranged to meet up with Clarissa and Anne at the *Louvre*. They arrived a little late, as their metro stop had exited directly into a mall parking garage that seemed to have no way out. After turning every corner, feeling like they would be trapped there forever, they finally found an escape route. (I imagine they must have been about as upset and flustered as I was when I got trapped at the SNCF.)

With both ordeals finally over, we totally cracked up about how incredibly ridiculous they had been. It seemed ironic to be as free as we've ever been in our lives, yet still trapped in a mall parking garage and at the SNCF.

We were still laughing hysterically when we ran into Melissa, our classmate in Ohio, who happened to be visiting Paris, too – small world!

After walking around the *Louvre*, we went to the *Pont Neuf*, to *Notre Dame*, then to a restaurant we'd found in the *Let's Go Europe* book. The description of the restaurant indicated you could get a three-course meal for only $8-$9, which is dirt cheap in France.

We were walking down the street looking for the place, when suddenly we looked up to see that we were already standing in front of it (!). The restaurant was overflowing with foreigners who had also found the place from a guidebook. It was decorated with chandeliers on the ceiling and animal heads on the walls. We sat under a peacock at a long table next to a couple from Australia.

Our waiter was incredibly loud but funny. The Australian couple kept asking him to talk more quietly, but he didn't seem to notice. I ordered a salad, chicken, and some peaches and sauce. The most amazing part of the whole meal was that we got free ice water, which you never find in Europe.

For the third course, we could select either dessert or cheese. Clarissa got a big hunk of *Camembert* with a pat of butter next to it. This struck us as absolutely hilarious, to think of eating that big hunk of cheese with butter on top of it and no bread.

The place was overflowing with even more people when we got up to leave. Kissing us each dramatically, the waiter thanked us for our vacating seats. Everyone in the room seemed to hear his booming voice and looked up to see what was going on.

Back at the hostel, a group of people from the U.K. and the U.S. invited us to join in on a game they were playing. When it's your turn, someone will stick a piece of paper on your forehead, attached by their spit. Then, you have to guess the name on your forehead.

After figuring out that the name on mine was "Jacques Chirac," I stepped away to call Jules, the exchange student we're meeting up with in Belgium. I talked with his mom, who told me to call back at midnight. Finally, I got a hold of him – on the fifth try. This was just in time, as he is meeting us later today at the train station in Brussels.

This morning, it was strange seeing Mike and Tom's empty room across the hall. They woke up early to catch the hovercraft to England, so we won't see them again until we're back in Freiburg. Now, we are on the train and on our way, too.

Clarissa and Anne both said they have been feeling frustrated and a little homesick because they can't speak French. As for me, I'm incredibly grateful to have had the chance to use my French over these past few days. There's more of it at our next stop, too.

Belgium…

Secrets from My Travel Diaries

> ➢ *The spirit of traveling young and free is a state of mind – it doesn't have to end.*

> ➢ *When in doubt, laugh!*

CHAPTER 7

Too Much of a Good Thing
(Belgium & Holland)

"This is my time to travel like I can only experience it now. . . Spend a day
in a city and then move on. . . Sightsee by day, go out by night..."

March 23, 1997

I find myself at a loss for how to describe my one and only night in Belgium. As I write this, we are speeding away from Brussels on yet another train, having decided we had enough of this particular adventure, as fun and, well, *interesting* as it was.

To set the stage for what I'm about to describe, I threw up in the train station while attempting to drink a Sprite, and the few bites of the croissant I just ate have been the first thing I've kept down all day. Clarissa and Anne each had to take a handle of my backpack and carry it through the station so that we could make our train. Otherwise, I probably wouldn't be sitting here right now.

Yesterday, as planned, Jules picked us up at the train station in his car, which was old and beat up but felt like a limo to us. It was so incredible to be picked up in a car after all the buses and trains and walking of the past month.

He asked us where we wanted to go, and we showed him in the *Let's Go* book, then we headed to the Grand Palace. On the way, we stopped to see the statue of the peeing boy and made a wish on some other statue nearby.

After that, we had waffles with whipped cream and chocolate, which were absolutely delicious and very typical of Belgium. Then we went to the king's palace. We wanted to go in and visit, not realizing that the king actually lived there. Jules was amused, not only that we wanted to go in, but that the king was literally in his palace at that time, as indicated by the flag on top of the building.

Next, we went to a place called the *Atomium*, which is the Belgian version of the Eiffel Tower in France. Basically, it is a huge building in the shape of an iron molecule, with comic strips everywhere on display. We saw "Mini-Europe," a depiction of Europe in miniature, down below but didn't go in because it cost $20 to get in, and the weather was awful.

Brussels is closer to the sea than Paris, and it's kept getting colder the further from Freiburg we get. It was about 5° Celsius (40° Fahrenheit), with a constant light rain that didn't let up all day. I definitely have gotten used to the warmth of Freiburg. You'd never know I'm from Ohio by how I was shivering in a long-sleeved shirt, sweatshirt, and two jackets.

Having seen the highlights in Brussels, which was lightning fast by car, we drove for about an hour to Jules's home in the small and beautiful town of Amay. The landscape was mostly farms and rolling hills, the grass incredibly lush and green.

At Jules's house, we watched TV for the first time since we arrived in Europe and were fascinated that it had channels in five different languages. (Belgium has sections of French, Flemish, and German-speaking people, all in one small country.)

We flipped back and forth from the German channel to an episode of *Melrose Place* in French, to a documentary on Prozac airing on the only channel in English. While we watched, I wrote a postcard to Fritz. He had specifically asked me to send him one from Brussels, because he said that with the formation of the European Union, it is being called the "Capital of Europe."

Jules cooked us dinner, making us a delicious meal of chicken with sauce and French fries. His mom came home then and was very sweet and warm to us. She spoke very little English, so I was the only one who really talked with her, while Clarissa and Anne chatted with Jules in English.

Jules's mom asked me about four times if we had gotten enough to eat and if it was good. I really wanted to just sit and talk with her for a while. She seemed like such a wonderful mom, and sometimes it's kind of nice to be around someone like that, especially when you are on your own, and your own mom is far away.

After dinner, we had beer at Jules' friend's house. Then, we dropped our stuff off at his sister's boyfriend's apartment. (Apparently, his sister's boyfriend doesn't live there anymore, because he moved into Jules's parent's house in Amay.)

At that point was when things really began to get strange. Jules came out wearing this funky hat with letters and signs all over it, with a chain hanging down from both sides. We asked him why in the world he was wearing it, and he said it was his ticket into some of the cooler clubs.

He took us out to his favorite bar. It was one o'clock in the morning, and the party was in full swing. The streets were so filled with people you could barely move, and people were peeing all over the streets. Most people were wearing these white, thin jackets like a doctor wears, covered with strange writing and symbols.

Jules and his friends were super nice, and we ended up having the best time. I was so exhilarated to be able to speak French, and after a few beers, I spoke nothing but French except to translate for my friends. A lot of the guys would come over and hit on us, and some were really forward. Jules and his friends looked out for us, though, and got rid of anyone unwanted.

Jules pointed out this one girl that he really liked and asked if I'd go talk to her for him. She and I ended up getting into an extended conversation outside the women's restroom, where she confided in me that she had had a boyfriend for the past four years, and the situation was "complicated." Eventually, I got Jules to come over and talk with us. I found her to be really cool, and it was fun orchestrating the whole thing in French.

Despite the wonderful time we had, when I woke up the next morning, smashed in on the couch next to Anne, I no longer felt so wonderful. Jules, his sister, and a couple of other friends took Clarissa and Anne out for Italian food for lunch. Somehow, Clarissa had locked her backpack and couldn't open it with the combination, so they stopped by a locksmith on the way there.

Jules wanted us to come back to the party that was going on all day and night today, but at that point, we'd had enough of Belgium. It was ironic to have partied so hard in Belgium that we had to take a train to Amsterdam, but that's what we did. At the train station, Jules asked if we'd had fun. I told him we'd had a great time but had to move on.

At the train station, I bought a stamp so I could send the postcard to Fritz. The nice man at the kiosk had to help me, as I couldn't even count my money; I was so out of it. I told him the Belgians I was with knew how to party harder than I did, to which he laughed and said he understood.

I slept most of the way on the train. When they announced the name of the border city between Belgium and Holland, Clarissa and Anne woke me up, thinking we had to switch trains there. They had to force the door open to get out of the train, which should have tipped us off that we were at the wrong place.

We stepped out onto the platform, only to find ourselves standing alone in the middle of nowhere, with no train station in sight. Fortunately, the conductor saw us and yelled for us to get back on the train. There was one more stop to go to connect to the train to Amsterdam.

The rest of the train ride was pretty uneventful. When we arrived in Amsterdam, we were freaked out because of all the stories we'd heard. We decided to stay in a Christian hostel, which was dirt cheap and claimed to be safe. (It's in the middle of the red-light district, but they said it was patrolled by cameras.)

Though the hostel was very close to the station, it took us a while to find it. I trailed behind Clarissa and Anne, as they figured out the logistics. At one point, one of them suggested we go into the 'arcade' to ask for directions, but then they realized it was actually a casino.

I'm writing this in our dorm room at the hostel. It's time to turn out my flashlight and get some sleep. Hopefully, the people watching soccer and yelling in the snack bar will shut up soon.

March 24, 1997

What an incredible day it has been in Amsterdam! I am feeling myself again – and very hungry. Luckily, there's good food everywhere and lots of cheese.

The Christian hostel seems out of place in the red-light district, but it turned out to be in a great location for sightseeing. When we walked out of our hostel this morning, we realized that we were about a block away from both the Sex Museum and the Marijuana Museum and close to pretty much everything else we'd wanted to see, too.

Our map was amazingly detailed and easy to follow. Nevertheless, on the way to Anne Frank's house, we walked too far and passed where we were supposed to turn. We turned back and ran into a group of French travelers, desperately asking for anyone who spoke their language. I tried to help them but had no idea how to find the place they were looking for. A few minutes later, we met a Scottish couple, also looking for the Anne Frank house. We walked with them and quickly found it.

I was truly captivated by the experience of being in the place where Anne Frank had lived and suffered. The whole time I felt like crying and walked around with tears in my eyes.

We got to see where the bookcase had hidden the family, watched a couple of short videos about it, and actually saw her first and second diaries. It was somehow so real being there. I felt as if I were taking a part of her with me as I walked out of each room.

After the Anne Frank House, we went to the Van Gogh Museum. When we got there, we realized that it was 13 guilders (almost $25 U.S.), so we didn't go in. On the way to the Jewish Museum, I ate a hot dog and later a piece of pizza. I was so hungry. Then, we went on a canal boat tour through Amsterdam's network of canals. It was incredible. The fact that we were only 16 miles away from the North Sea amazed me.

The tour guide on the canal boat repeated the tour three times in Flemish, English, and French. I enjoyed listening to each of the three languages, and the repetition was helpful because it was hard to hear anything. A big group of Italians across from us were talking loudly the whole time. The only time they got quiet was when we passed by a floating coffee shop. They all grabbed their cameras and furiously photographed it.

On this trip, I've learned that so much of what I thought I'd lost of my French has been in my head all along. Because of their similarities to other languages

I've learned, I can even recognize some of the words in Flemish, Spanish, and Italian. I truly believe there is nothing in the world like studying another language, as it has opened a world to me that I could never have imagined.

After the canal boat tour, we went to the Sex Museum, which we heard was a "must-see" in Amsterdam. We felt a little strange because we were among the only women in the whole place. In one of the small rooms, there was a big screen showing two people getting intimate, which was playing in a sort of slow motion. We ended up standing there watching the screen for quite a while. Guys kept drifting in and out of the room, and somehow, we were still there. Finally, we asked ourselves why on earth we were still watching it and left.

Outside the museum, we passed by erotic shops all along the road. There were women standing in the windows with only underwear on, waiting for their next client to come by. A guy standing outside a sex shop asked us if we wanted a job. Someone else offered us Ecstasy.

We checked out the Marijuana Museum, then went into one of the infamous coffee shops we'd seen everywhere. The menu had about 20 different kinds of drugs on it. We debated ordering a space cake, discreetly opening up *Let's Go* to read the section about them. *Let's Go* indicated that the contents of the space cakes are unregulated, and eating one could cause paralysis.

I guess the trip to the coffee shop explained a lot. Ever since we arrived, the hostel has felt like it was in some kind of time warp. Back at the hostel, the same guys who had been playing pool since we got here were still playing. And the people who have been sleeping in our dorm room, seemingly day and night, were still there in their beds.

Now, it's time to close this diary as I sit here in my bunk on our last night in Amsterdam. As I do so, I feel an overwhelming sense of amazement and gratitude for all that I have experienced today.

March 25, 1997

We woke up early to catch the Heineken brewery tour, which started at nine-thirty in the morning. After getting lost on the way, we ended up having to run the rest of the way to make it on time.

The tour was only 2 guilders [about $4] and got us unlimited beer and these awesome, twisty corn chips and cheese. It took us through the history of Heineken and how it was made. The tour concluded at a large bar, where you could drink all you could hold until eleven o'clock in the morning. We devoured both our basket of twisty corn chips and cheese and the one on the empty table next to us.

At eleven o'clock, when the tour ended, we walked around the city, taking pictures and feeling buzzed. Then, we hopped a train to Zaanse Schans, a little village outside of Amsterdam. It was the most adorable little town, with small shops, five windmills lining the coastline, a cheese factory, and a chocolate factory.

At one of the shops, this guy showed us how he made wooden shoes, which Holland is famous for. We tried to go into the chocolate factory, but they only made the powder and didn't give tours.

The cheese factory was small and family-owned and produced something like 500 different kinds of cheese. A lady dressed in traditional attire told us all about cheese and the process of making it. We tried all the free samples and ordered cheese sandwiches with mustard. (After all that cheese, we wanted nothing to do with any other cheese for the rest of the day.)

Having stuffed ourselves with cheese, we couldn't fit in another bite – until we found the Dutch pancakes and wanted to try them, too. We ran around, hoping to get hungry again, and finally split one between us before heading back to Amsterdam.

On the way back to Amsterdam, we nearly boarded the train that was going in the opposite direction but realized it in time. Then, we stopped by a grocery store to use up the last of our Dutch currency, which would be worthless to us in a matter of hours.

Now, we face yet another night train and about 11 hours of travel to get back to Freiburg. With both tiredness and total and complete happiness descending upon me, I will end this diary entry.

Secrets from My Travel Diaries

➢ *Part of growing up is about exploring the world and setting your own boundaries.*

➢ *Having friends you can count on is gold.*

➢ *There is such a thing as too much cheese.*

CHAPTER 8

Learning Without Opening a Book
(Zurich & Back to Freiburg)

"I think I would have learned more studying abroad if I hadn't had to study."

March 26, 1997

On the train, we found an empty car that was made for six people. It was a real find because the rest of the cars were full. Then, we realized that the seats folded out into beds and decided it didn't get any better than that. I went straight to sleep, waking up periodically in the night.

Around three-thirty in the morning, a bunch of drunk men boarded the train and were really loud. One of them opened the door to our car, wearing black leather, and asked us where we were from. We were so groggy that we misunderstood and said "Amsterdam." He studied us for a few more minutes, said, "You are Americans" in English, and left.

We decided we might as well put the 24 hours on our Eurail passes to full use, so we didn't get off at the Freiburg stop. Instead, we stayed on the train and spent the day in Zurich. This was perhaps a stupid idea, judging from how tired we were, but at least we got our money's worth.

In Basel, two conductors appeared and told us in Swiss German that we had to change trains. So, we changed trains again, rode another hour to Zurich, and got ready for the new day by washing our faces and brushing our teeth on the train.

Once in Zurich, Anne took off to stay the night with her Swiss relatives. Meanwhile, Clarissa and I put our bags in lockers and got a good map. We were on our own without *Let's Go* for the day. Not expecting to go to Zurich, we hadn't ripped those pages out of the book and taken them with us.

We had barely any money to change, and everything was so expensive, so we basically just wandered down the street with the map. There were all kinds of shops and points of interest, just south of the train station. We explored some of the churches but didn't go in because there was a wedding about to take place in one, and the others looked boarded up and most were locked.

Once we found ourselves outside of the range of the map, we turned back and went down to *Zürichsee* [Lake Zurich] to soak up the sunshine. Unfortunately, it was not as warm as we had hoped, though.

We were excited when we found a boat that would take us around the lake for free with our Eurail passes. Unfortunately, the boat turned out to be more like transportation and not a tour. People kept getting off and on at different stops, and they never gave us any history or background about the lake.

We felt about as exhausted as the woman sitting next to us, who slept the entire way around the lake, never opening her eyes the whole time. After riding the entire hour-long route back to where we started, we headed for the train station.

In Basel, we missed our connecting train. We pooled together our remaining francs and shared 2,90 (about $2) Swiss francs' worth of a very hard – but very edible – baguette. Then, we spent the rest of the hour sitting in an exhausted stupor, waiting for the next train to arrive.

It feels good to be back in Freiburg now – at least for a couple of days before we leave again for Easter week. I didn't realize how much I missed it until we got back to Clarissa's apartment. All the same familiar faces were in the kitchen, playing a game called *Tabu* [Tabou], and it felt like a reunion. Mike and Tom agreed that it seemed like an eternity since we'd seen each other.

We spent the evening trading stories about our vacations and trying to decide what courses we should take. (The pre-program German immersion is over, and the official semester at the university starts tomorrow.)

Now, I'm back at my apartment, struggling to stay awake, as my parents are supposed to call me. They got a new offer to call Germany for $0.35/minute that they are going to try out.

March 27, 1997

I was sound asleep when my parents called last night, after having spent the day with my grandparents. When I talked with them, I felt a combination of homesickness and culture shock, possibly because of all the countries I've been in over the past couple of weeks.

It's been a letdown coming back from our travels. I've been exhausted and confused about which classes to take. It's unsettling to have no idea what direction my life should go in these next few months. I'm not used to having so many choices.

I just sat through a class called *Germany as an Economic Power*. When I first heard about it, I was really excited, but now I'm so out of the groove that I have no desire to go to class and study. It is so much easier in the U.S., where everything is familiar. Here, everything is different and fascinating, and I just want to be in the middle of it all.

We have a grace period before we have to finalize our class schedule so that we have time to sample different classes. I'm glad we have that opportunity because I attended a class earlier that I have absolutely no desire to attend again.

I talked with one of the full-year students, who gave me the scoop about which classes to take and which to avoid. It was so helpful. I want to learn as much as I can and have an awesome semester without doing lots of studying. You've got to take the right classes in order to achieve that.

Adding to the complication with my schedule is that I need to pick up at least one French class toward my minor. The best option seems to be a French conversation class called *Hören und Sprechen* [Hear and Speak]. Our main assignments are to read the French newspaper once a week and to do listening and transcribing exercises in the *Sprachlabor* [speaking lab].

I also decided to try out a French literature class about my favorite French author, Marcel Proust. It was pretty intimidating, as most of the local students are very advanced, on a whole other level. Plus, the French literature courses are conducted in German, which might make me lose my mind.

It's so strange how relaxed the local professors seem to be, compared to the ones in the U.S. When I got to the literature class, there was a note on the door saying that the professor would be arriving an hour late.

I spent that hour sitting on a bench outside the door, writing in my diary, and watching students walk by, read the sign, and leave. When the class finally started, it did seem like an interesting way to meet local students, though I'm still not sure if I can handle Marcel Proust in German.

Hilda happened to be on the bus when I boarded it back to *Merzhauserstraße*. We sat and talked all the way back, and then she asked if I wanted to go with her to have a drink at the bar.

I hesitated at first, because I'd been planning to do some prep work for my classes. Hilda responded that while class is important, "*Du bist nur einmal in Deutschland*" [You are only in Germany once.]

And so, of course, I had to go with her then – and I'm glad I did!

Secrets from My Travel Diaries

> ➢ *"Getting your money's worth" may not be worth it, if you're too exhausted to enjoy it.*

> ➢ *Deciding from many options is harder than navigating just a few.*

> ➢ *Get done what you need to, but take every opportunity to live your life.*

CHAPTER 9

Dreams Come True
(Barcelona, French Riviera, Italy)

"Our travels have been like a fairy tale, or maybe more like a commercial for Italian coffee. Somehow, I've left the real world and landed in a whole new one – filled with beautiful sites, wonderful friendships, and incredible experiences."

March 28, 1997

It's eight o'clock in the morning, and we are on our final leg to Barcelona after a long series of train rides. The sun is shining, and we are passing by palm trees and cacti on what I think is the Spanish Riviera.

There is beauty all around me, and I'm just marveling at how unimaginably grateful I am to be here. Every single day fills me with happiness and fascination. What an incredible life this is. Each time the door of the next train opens, a whole new part of the world awaits us to explore.

A few stops ago, some Swiss guys got on the train, singing at the top of their lungs and drinking beer. There are about a dozen guys and a few girls. Apparently, they're headed to Barcelona for some training, as they're enlisting in the Swiss army (which is compulsory for men in Switzerland).

As I try to write, a few of them are swarming around Clarissa and Anne, offering them beer, talking to them in French, and periodically bursting into song.

March 30, 1997

Barcelona, Spain

It is evening on Easter Sunday, and we are again on a train, this time speeding away from Barcelona. I don't know how I'm going to catch up with all that has happened in the past couple of days.

I've got the time, though, because we have an incredibly long train ride to Nice on the French Riviera. This time we didn't splurge for the *couchette*, either, so we'll be sitting up the whole time. (A *couchette* is a small compartment with bunk beds.)

At least this train ride is not quite as long as the one to Barcelona. Getting to Barcelona took us about 16 hours. We had connections in Basel and Geneva; an overnight train to Portbou, Spain; a two-hour layover in Portbou (at five-thirty in the morning), then another two-hour train ride to get there.

Traveling during Easter week is definitely an experience. When we boarded the train in Geneva, we got on the wrong car. The train was already moving by the time we figured out that our car number was about ten cars away. We had to maneuver through swarms of people with our huge backpacks, trying to find the right car, which was extremely annoying.

We were glad we sprang for the *couchette* for the nine-hour overnight stretch. We shared ours with two Spanish women and found it to be really comfortable; we actually got some real sleep on it.

The two-hour wait in the station at Portbou, in the wee hours of the morning, was actually pretty fun. We felt surprisingly awake after a decent night's sleep in the *couchette*. And with two hours on our hands to hang out in the station with lots of other travelers, we got some good travel advice.

This brings us back to where I left off before when we were on the train heading to Barcelona. The train was quiet until the group from the Swiss military got on board. Though I found them really annoying at first, they ended up being totally hilarious and kind of made the trip for us. We ended up hanging out with them on and off the entire time we were there.

When we finally got to Barcelona, we stopped by our hostel to shower and drop off our bags. The hostel was very clean, had frilly bedspreads on the beds, and no curfew. The only downside was that there was no free breakfast. We shared our room with two other Americans and an Australian but never got much of a chance to talk with them because they went to bed and got up early, and we did the opposite.

As advertised in our guidebook, the hostel was pretty much in the middle of all the action, down a small side street from the main drag, *Las Ramblas*. Anne had been to Spain before, but Clarissa and I had never visited anywhere remotely tropical. The mood along *Las Ramblas* was so vibrant and full of life and was like nothing we'd ever seen before. It was a wonderful introduction to Spain.

There was a seemingly endless line of street vendors on *Las Ramblas*. Dancers and entertainers were everywhere. The cafe – and restaurant – lined streets flowed with a constant stream of people, as far as you could see. Against all odds, we ran into Melissa, our classmate from Ohio, a second time in two weeks. (What?!)

After checking out the vendors' wares along the street, we found a café and shared a pitcher of the typical Spanish drink, *sangria*. Clarissa and I had never even heard of it, but signs for it were everywhere. Anne had been to Barcelona before and was our guide to interpret such things.

The energy of the place was incredible. The whole time it felt like we were living large, too. Because of the exchange rate with the *Peseta,* everything seemed so incredibly cheap, especially the food and taxis. It felt so freeing after having visited so many other, much more expensive countries.

Through the haze of the *sangria,* everything going around us seemed even more vibrant than it had before. Not far down the road, we happened upon the group from the Swiss army that we'd met on the train. They were sitting at an outdoor café drinking more beers and waved us over. We arranged to meet up with them that evening outside the cathedral near our hostel.

When we went to the cathedral that evening, though, it turned out that about half the city was there, too. It was Good Friday, and there was a massive parade outside. There were people everywhere, some of them wheeling carts with huge replicas of Jesus and Mary, some playing in bands, and others walking alongside, singing and praying. We ended up taking in the parade in amazement, never finding the Swiss army group.

A little while later, we went to *Port Olympico* to check out the nightlife. As we were ordering a drink, they all walked in the door. I was feeling tired from the long train ride, and that's when my energy came back. It was fun to be innocently hit on by them, with no other expectations, knowing that in a couple of days, we'd all be moving on (definitely a confidence-builder after the whole situation with Fritz, which was still a sore spot).

The funniest thing was sitting there with a whole table full of glasses of beer they'd ordered, listening to Simone try to sweet-talk Anne. He could speak a little German, but filled in with French whatever words he didn't know. They had quite a few problems communicating and kept calling over to me, asking me to translate.

The next couple of days, we alternated between sightseeing, hanging out with the group from Switzerland, and doing both at the same time. Time just seemed to flow in Barcelona at a different pace than in Germany – and anywhere else I'd ever been before. You couldn't speed it up or slow it down; it just went at its pace. (The only thing that got a little annoying was that it took forever to pay the bill at restaurants.)

One afternoon we got tired from walking and just sat on a bench, watching some of the tour groups go by, trying to guess what country people were from. This time of traveling and living in Freiburg has shed some major light for me about myself and other cultures. If I had to leave tomorrow, I'd know that I've already expanded my horizons so much (but I'm glad I don't have to!).

On Saturday night, we wanted to see a flamenco dance performance because Anne said it was typical of the region and a "must-see." The only thing was that the tickets were really expensive, at 4,200 *pesetas* (about $35).

We found out we could get discounted tickets by waiting until everyone with reservations had been seated and filling in whichever seats were available. Unfortunately, by that time, we'd missed the first 20 minutes of a show that wasn't that much longer. What I did see was mesmerizing, though. Women in bright, flowing dresses danced in seemingly effortless cadence with their partners, their black-heeled feet stomping to a tantalizing rhythm.

The next morning was Easter Sunday. It was our last day in Barcelona before moving on to Nice. We got up after only a few hours of sleep and went back to the cathedral. It didn't feel like Easter, with everything so unfamiliar. I felt really disconnected at the service because I didn't understand anything the priest was saying. Also, there were tourists in jeans wandering through the cathedral throughout the service, taking pictures.

The rest of the day didn't feel like Easter, either. Most of the Swiss military group had crashed out by then, but a few of them, including Simone (who was still really into Anne), met up with us. We went for lunch and sightseeing at Poble Español, a village with traditional architecture from all over Spain.

By the end of the day, I felt as if I couldn't even talk or think anymore in any language. I guess that was my signal that it was time to move on. Now, we just have to make it through the long train ride to Nice, sitting up all night, surrounded by a bunch of American tourists. I'm getting culture shock hearing them chatting all around us.

April 1, 1997
Nice, French Riviera, France

It's almost nine o'clock at night. I'm sharing Clarissa's top bunk in our *couchette*, as my bunk is on the bottom and is claustrophobic and cramped.

I'm glad this is our last night train of the trip, though I did get some decent sleep in the last *couchette*, so hopefully I will again. This time, we're sharing a car with an Italian man in a business suit and a Filipino woman who's already asleep in her bunk.

As the train slowly pulls away from Nice and we head off to Rome, I again feel hopelessly behind in my writing. That is despite having written for a straight 2 1/2 hours only a couple of days ago on the train over here. Every day is so much fun, I can barely keep up.

At times I feel so tired I can barely write, but I still have to do it. Writing has been important to me since I learned how, and it feels like pouring out on these pages is what helps me think things through. Honestly, I can't even imagine how some people go through life without a diary to capture their thoughts – and the little (and big!) things that happen in their lives.

Anyway, back to arriving in Nice... The train pulled in around eight in the morning. I ended up sleeping much better than expected, curled up in the seat. (I guess the trick is to get yourself so tired that you can pretty much sleep anywhere.)

When we got to the hostel, the guy asked if anyone could speak French. Then, he told me that he'd run out of dormitories and wanted to offer us a private room with a balcony instead for the same price. It was wonderful to have a private room – and with a balcony – for the first time ever. The only downside was that our room wasn't ready for another few hours, and there was nowhere to wash up and brush our teeth.

Walking down the street, we found a McDonald's, which was the first time we'd been in one since we started traveling. There, we realized that not only could we use the bathroom to wash up, we could also get a great breakfast of pancakes, an English muffin, coffee, and orange juice for only 17 francs [about $3].

The only bad part about McDonald's was that a backpacker saw that we were from the U.S., too, and started telling us about getting robbed in Spain. She went on and on and started to freak us out. We got out of there as quickly as we could.

On the way back to the hostel, we went to the Russian Cathedral. Then, we passed by a beautiful fountain and wanted to get a picture. We had to keep waiting for the fountain to come back on between each picture because it was on some kind of timer. Hopefully, at least one of the photos will come out when we get the film developed in Freiburg.

While walking through *Vieux Nice* [Historic Nice], I got my first glimpse of the sugar-white shores and breathtaking blue waters I'd seen in the photos. We kept walking down the hill and through the tiny streets of *Vieux Nice*, trying to get there, getting completely trapped in the maze of streets, but finally found it.

We were determined to lay out on the beach and soak up the sun. However, the French Riviera up close was not quite as I pictured it. The beach was all chalky white rock instead of sand. We attempted to lay out on the beach, anyway. The rocks were not only a bit uncomfortable, but also left us totally covered with white dust.

Eventually, we found a place to rent lounge chairs and spent the rest of the afternoon basking in the spring sun. I used my green fleece jacket as a pillow again, as I did in my first days in Freiburg and on many overnight train rides. With the sun shining and the ocean breeze, I didn't need much else.

A little later, after combing the beach for a bathroom, we found a portable one. The door would lock behind you when you walked out. Then you'd hear the swish of a disinfection cycle for what seemed like forever before you could open it again.

We experimented with whether we could save coins by keeping the door slightly open for the next person and sliding through. However, the sensors kicked off the disinfection process anyway. Poor Anne was in line of the stream and had to jump out of the way.

On our walk to the beach, we caught sight of a restaurant with a huge sign saying they'd give you a free birthday cake for your birthday. This was perfect timing, as it was Clarissa's 21st birthday on April 1st – April Fool's Day. (Turning 21 doesn't mean the same thing in Europe as it does in the U.S., but we wanted to do our best to give it the importance it would have at home.)

We returned at dinnertime, and Clarissa showed her I.D. to get the free cake. It took a while to get our server to believe that the day and month are written opposite in the U.S. Finally, she relented, and Clarissa got a fabulous-looking chocolate cake with a sparkler on top of it.

Afterward, we went out for karaoke. We picked some cool songs, like "Sugar Sugar," "The Tide Is High," and, of course, "Happy Birthday." There weren't that many people there, so we got a lot of chances to sing. We met a couple of German businessmen, Joachim and Klaus, and spoke with them in German for most of the night. They bought us a couple of rounds, and we sang some karaoke. Joachim's rendition of "Hello," by Lionel Ritchie, sounded hilarious.

Joachim kept telling me I was so *"süß"* [sweet], that I had the prettiest smile, and that I smiled so much more often than German women do. He's right, I guess: Americans *do* seem to smile a lot more. That doesn't necessarily mean we're happier or more authentic, though. I think we smile because we're *taught* to smile through it all, no matter what.

Maybe in other cultures where they smile less, they're showing how they really feel. I'd never given much thought to that before, which goes to show how much you learn about yourself and others when studying abroad.

Anyway, on our last night on the French Riviera, Clarissa had a great birthday. And even though it wasn't in Germany, but in France, I have now kissed a German.

April 2, 1997
Rome, Italy

Our hostel in Rome is a total pit – and expensive, in comparison to the others we've stayed in. There are only two bathrooms and three showers for everyone in the hostel, and they quickly run out of hot water. When it was finally our turn, the whole bathroom floor was swimming with water. We thought about finding another hostel, but we just decided to deal with it since we're only here for a few days.

Walking through Rome and the Vatican felt like walking through history. There seemed to be historical things on every corner, but unfortunately, we didn't know what most of them were.

The paintings at the Sistine Chapel were so lifelike; it seemed as though they were about to get up and walk right off the walls. I wanted to spend all day just staring up at the ceiling, but the place was overflowing with Easter week travelers.

Between my fascination and the crowds everywhere, I managed to lose Clarissa and Anne and asked a guard if there was another exit. At first, he couldn't understand me, so he took me to someone else, who told me in broken English: "One exit. Must come out sometime."

Meanwhile, Clarissa and Anne had been waiting for me inside, where they'd run into a couple of people from our program in Freiburg and a guy we met in Amsterdam. Much to my relief, they did eventually come out.

While at the Coliseum, we met another traveler who tipped us off to put in 500 lire (about $0.30) to light up the famous statue of Moses, sculpted by Michelangelo, at Saint Peter in Chains Cathedral. When we lit him up, people all around began frantically taking pictures.

One day, I felt a nudge to find a pyramid that I kept seeing from afar. It stuck out amidst the Roman architecture, and I learned it had been dedicated to the city by the U.S. Army. Clarissa and Anne weren't up for going, so I went by myself to find it, leaving them at the *Plaza de Porta Capena*.

On our own in this foreign city, during the space of an hour, each of us had an experience that was all our own. I followed a wall all the way to its end and found the pyramid, feeling this incredible freedom and independence, wandering alone through the streets of Rome.

Meanwhile, Anne sat and thought and had a sort of catharsis about who she was and what she wanted in life. And Clarissa took the best nap of her life, full of vivid dreams, in the middle of the grass.

SECRETS FROM MY TRAVEL DIARIES

It's hard to explain what those experiences meant, except for this incredible feeling of being able to do whatever you chose. For the first time in our lives, no one on earth knew exactly where we were – not even each other.

On our last evening, we went to dinner at a place recommended in *Let's Go*, that had great pasta for a cheap price. When we walked in the door, we immediately noticed a large table of very good-looking Italian guys. We ordered the touristic dinner and thoroughly enjoyed each course as it arrived. The tortellini was the best ever.

Toward the end of the meal, the guys started talking to us, and a couple of them came over to our table. I was instantly enamored by a guy named Gian Luca. Ironically, Anne liked a guy named Simone (the same name as the guy from Switzerland, just an Italian translation). Clarissa's crush was named Fabricio.

All of them were serving their compulsory tour in the Italian army. Their curfew was eleven o'clock in the evening, and the barracks were an hour away, so we didn't have much time, but we made the most of it.

We spent the rest of the evening walking arm in arm through the streets of Rome. Gian Luca led me down the street, protecting me from oncoming cars and hanging on every word I said (even though I don't know if he had any idea what I was saying).

As we walked down the street, he pointed things out, teaching me the words in Italian and singing me the songs he knew in English. He made me feel beautiful… like a princess… put on a pedestal. I was thoroughly charmed. With Gian Luca, I had this feeling of floating, like nothing could ever happen to me with him there.

At the end of the night, we walked them to the train station. Gian Luca said that they would have to stay in the barracks "for a very long time" if they didn't make their curfew, but invited me to meet up again on the weekend, when he was free again. "We go in *Roma*," he said.

I really wished I could have seen Gian Luca again. Part of me wanted nothing more than to stay. Instead we kissed in the middle of the train station before they caught their train, and they gave us their home addresses even though we all know we wouldn't write.

It strikes me that in this whirlwind we're on, there is this incredible euphoria of experiencing something new and exciting on every corner. Yet, in the undercurrents, I cannot shake this wistful, anchorless feeling – a tug in another direction entirely.

I felt incredibly drawn to Gian Luca – yet the choice to move on is like an undertow that pulls me away. Moving on – not getting too attached – is always more compelling – especially when it means traveling with my friends. . .

We floated on a cloud down the road – until we realized we were lost, and then we asked for directions, first at a McDonald's and again at an ice cream shop. Eventually, we found our hostel.

I woke up at six o'clock in the morning singing "How do you solve a problem like Maria?" from *The Sound of Music,* and dreaming of Gian Luca. I had been having such vivid dreams – with images of nuns and ancient ruins and Gian Luca's face coursing through my subconscious. We have never known what to expect anywhere we've been, and this has been the most wonderful time I could ever have imagined. . .

April 5, 1997

Florence, Italy

We arrived at the train station a little late because McDonald's had taken too long to make our pancakes. When we finally got there, there was no sign to

"Venice" anywhere. We finally asked a policeman, who informed us that the train had been canceled because of a strike. After a flurry of running from ticket window to information booth to money exchange window, we hopped on a train to Florence instead – such a wonderfully unexpected twist, as we would have missed it otherwise!

Whereas Rome seemed more like a big city, with a lot of ancient ruins and nuns and clergymen around, when I saw the view of Florence, my first thought was, "*This* is Italy!" I can't even describe the feeling. I think it's just something you have to experience: to be standing in the middle of Florence, surrounded by its beauty.

My favorite part of Florence was the famous domed church, the Florence Cathedral. I guess I liked it because it was actually made up of three random parts that were unattached, and it looked completely different up close than I'd imagined.

The other best part of Florence was the ice cream (called *gelato*). All three of us had two gelatos that day, with three flavors each. We decided it was the creamiest, most savory ice cream we'd ever eaten.

At night, we went to a lookout point to see Florence lit up, but it was cloudy and the view didn't do it justice. We stayed up there awhile anyway, reflecting on the experiences we've shared, that it feels like no one at home could understand. It's as if I'm in a dream.

April 6, 1997 – 6:45 AM

It's been a tough morning so far. We got up very early to leave for the train station to go to Venice. Clarissa began the day throwing up (we thought it was likely to be too much gelato), but we managed to get packed up and ready.

When we tried to leave, we found that we were locked in the hostel until six o'clock in the morning. The lady at the hostel got violently furious at us when we tried to get out early. I don't think ever in my life have I seen anyone so spitfire mad. We got out of there quickly, the first chance we got.

April 6, 1997 – 11:30 PM

Venice, Italy

I find it amazing that Venice was built with wood on top of the water and that there are no cars at all. There were little canals everywhere, all stemming from the Grand Canal and going every which way. The narrow, windy streets were lined with shops full of tourists from all over the world.

Maps are pretty useless in Venice. Basically, all you can do is just wind through the narrow roads, across bridges and little *piazzas* [open squares], and continue in the general direction you want to go, as best you can. We spent the day going on a boat ride and visiting places such as St. Marco Square. (I did *not* like all the pigeons landing on me.)

We really wanted to go on a gondola, but at 80,000 lire [about $50], we needed to find someone who would go with us to share the cost. I stopped people on the street, speaking all three languages I knew, along with the bits of Italian I learned from Gian Luca. No luck.

Venice is a very romantic city, but it has a different vibe than Rome and Florence and seems to mainly attract older tourists. It's probably better to come back here later in life when I am older, married, and have more money.

We now have about eight more hours until we get to Freiburg, with layovers and stops. My nose is stuffed up, I'm tired, and my clothes are covered with layers of filth from smoky bars and dust from the French Riviera. None of that matters, though.

Rooted in the everyday pressures at home, I couldn't have imagined all that I'm experiencing now. My feet are not planted anywhere. I come and go as I please, and I have the most amazing friends who go with me. There is always something else new and exciting awaiting us.

Everywhere we go, we create incredible memories, but it's not just that. There's something more that I'm taking back with me, and it's nothing that will weigh down my suitcase on the way home. It's a change in my perceptions, an expanded view of the world. And it's an understanding of different viewpoints and cultures acquired by traveling and experiencing.

Anne said that this week has been magical because everything she wished for has come true. It feels like our experience has been right out of a commercial for Italian coffee.

In some ways, I wish I could go back again and relive this entire dream. Then again, I would only want to do that if I could start completely over, with the exact thoughts and perspectives I had when I left. To do anything else would completely change the experience.

Secrets from My Travel Diaries

- ➢ *Every place you go has a different vibe and energy; sometimes you just have to soak up the sun!*

- ➢ *Embracing the unexpected makes space for your dreams to come true.*

- ➢ *Travel can change you, and shift your perspective.*

- ➢ *What was there before that was WRONG is this:*

CHAPTER 10

My 20s: "You can do anything!"

"I am no longer satisfied to just hear about places. I have an insatiable desire to see other parts of the world for myself – and experience what they have to offer." – 1997

April 7, 2022

I pause from writing and get up from my computer. My mind is racing, and I need a break.

What an unexpected form of reverse mentorship this is. This lens into the past is refracting a future that is like an open canvas. Each day of this new life is beginning to feel like the door of those trains opening – to new places, new adventures, and new possibilities.

It feels like I've been starting each day painting on yesterday's canvas, the paint lingering with the heavy undertone of past mistakes. . . disappointments. . . things I wish I'd done.

But what if yesterday's canvas were already complete, ready to hang up with the others, in this mosaic of Life? And what if, by letting go, the dawn could weave a brand new one – a fresh canvas on which to paint whatever I choose?

This is a massive shift in my perspective.

I flip randomly through my diary and land on the words: *"My life is here in Freiburg, at least for these next precious months."*

I can feel the gratitude exuding through the page.

Precious. Yes, that's it. . . Over the years, I've forgotten that my time is precious.

I've got to start remembering again.

It feels like my entire life is reflecting back to me, like on one of those slide projectors my parents used to chronicle their vacations. The decades of my life since those diaries were written are reemerging, woven together in themes.

I lay aside my diaries, my computer, my phone – and walk to the forest. Free of devices, and left only with the one in my head, I feel lighter, as I walk down the path through the trees.

Stopping in the middle of the trail, I look up and take in the scenery. I've always loved how the light shines through the trees. A flowing motion surrounds me, as the trees and branches sway in a gentle breeze.

I'm struck by a catharsis of my own, like Anne had on that hill in Rome … The trees, like the sails on a boat, don't brace themselves against the wind – they move with it.

The tides don't struggle against the forces of nature, or try to be something they aren't, either. They just flow – in and out, in and out.

Nor does the sun labor over whether to reappear over the horizon in the morning. Day after day, it stretches anew across the sky, its aura of colors painting the horizon like an angel spreading her wings across the sky.

Meanwhile, I've been struggling. . . and grasping. . . and resisting. I've been bracing myself against the winds and the tide, doubling down on being who I'm not. . . trying to want what I do not. . . pushing against time.

Drifting away, without an anchor, I've become disconnected from what's most important to me.

Why? How did I get here?

I guess I was caught up in the flurry of, "You can do anything." It swept me up like a tornado.

Over and over again growing up, people told me, "You can do anything." It was all said with the best of intentions, to encourage me. However, my interpretation of what it meant became like a script, programmed in my brain. It became my truth and my approach to life.

The highlight reel of my 20s reflects back to me. The theme for that decade? "I can do anything." I *could* do anything. . . and I pretty much did.

I pulled it off the same as I wrote in my diaries: by keeping life uncomplicated, always moving, not getting too attached.

"I thought I might lose you to another company, but I never expected to lose you to the Peace Corps." Those were my manager's words when I sat across from him at his desk that day.

It was three years after graduation. I was turning in my resignation from my first job and heading to Nicaragua with the Peace Corps. He was surprised. The people who knew me well were not.

The fact was, I'd been dreaming about going somewhere warm and Spanish-speaking since Freiburg. When I graduated, though, the economy was rocking. I hustled to pursue every opportunity and landed multiple job offers.

When the time came to decide on one, I did the sensible thing: I took the opportunity I liked best.

The position I chose was a coveted one: Territory Sales Manager in Chicago, northern Illinois, and southern Wisconsin. I had my own company car, budget, and book of business. Clarissa and I joined the company together and spent the first three months in sales and product training, traveling together around the U.S. and Canada.

The field I'd chosen was relationship-based, industrial, and male-dominated. It was the perfect fit for someone like me: I could do anything, and I'd spent my life admiring my industrial engineer father. I loved seeing how things were made, and I loved making things happen.

Despite the courage I'd fostered in Europe, I was nervous about moving to Chicago by myself. I remember driving there from Ohio, my car loaded to the brim. Night fell, and as I turned a corner, the Chicago city skyline appeared, larger than life. Instantly, an electric excitement replaced my fear, and I knew that I was on my way.

Chicago was good for me. I had a great sales territory, colleagues, and mentors. Visitors poured in from Ohio on the weekends, and I developed local friendships, too. Gas prices were $1 per gallon, and you could go anywhere. Flights were cheap, and you could breeze through the airport without taking off your shoes. I felt free.

But I also had this persistent feeling, like running after a train that had already left the station. I'd listen to the radio as I drove all over the state, calling on clients. Working for a traditional company – what I'd always imagined I'd do – felt like a different universe from the startups I kept hearing about.

I spent New Year's Eve 2000 in downtown Chicago, making the rounds at parties. We all figured if the world was about to end, we might as well be out enjoying ourselves. At the stroke of midnight, the party continued; after all that hype, the climax did not come.

Life was good in Chicago, but I began to long for some other adventure, for some other way to feel free. The dream of going into the Peace Corps began to rise up again. Being able to break free and go there was a welcome reprieve from, *"Never again will you be this free."*

All signs began to indicate that it was time to go. My cohort at work had already begun to flee, including Clarissa, who decided to get married and stay in Ohio. This was pivotal for me, as I thought we would be on the same path forever.

Without her, I felt alone on my own island, but I kept going anyway. One of my primary motivations was getting out of that climate. I was incredibly tired of the cold. And the summer of 2000 never got warm.

The coming of summer had always been a lighthouse in the darkness of winter, ever since I was a kid. The lake effect chill hovered, all through June, July, and August, as if forcing me out.

My cousin visited me in the height of the July heat that wasn't. All she could talk about for months was going sunbathing on the beach at Lake Michigan. We even tried it. But after sitting on the beach in our bathing suits for a while, we had to admit, through chattering teeth, that it was just too cold.

Jimmy Buffett sang, *"I Wanna Go Where It's Warm."* I rewound that song and pressed play again and again as I planned my getaway.

I was very close to my grandmother and visited her every weekend I could. However, in the year 2000, she passed away. It felt like she was giving me permission to leave the country again. I continued taking Spanish classes at night and applied to the Peace Corps.

One snowy afternoon, a letter arrived, notifying me that I'd been assigned to the Small Business Development Sector in Nicaragua. At that time, the news was abuzz about the dot-com bust and the corporate scandals.

There was nothing keeping me in the U.S. anymore. I was free to realize the dream I'd discovered in Freiburg: to learn Spanish and live in Latin America. It was 2001, and I was on my way again.

The first few months in Nicaragua, I took community-based language immersion near Managua. Then, I was assigned a post in Jinotega, in the lush, mountainous coffee country in the northernmost department of the country. There, I spent my two years of service teaching business skills to small business owners, microfinance loan officers, and high school vocational students.

Upon my return from the Peace Corps, I rode another wave. In 2004 I fulfilled my dream to attend the Thunderbird School of Global Management in Arizona. And I spent the hot, dusty Arizona summer of that year studying abroad in Guadalajara, Mexico.

The director of the Guadalajara program encouraged me and even recommended me to companies and helped me get interviews. I accepted a position, took my last coursework in South America, and traveled from Argentina to Ecuador. Then, I moved to Houston, Texas, to begin my corporate career.

Joining corporate America felt like a solid career. I didn't question the path that I was blazing. There was no need to. I could do anything, no matter what. I knew that for certain, with unshakable faith. And if it was hard, it was okay. I had grown up with the belief that life was supposed to be hard, so I was up for the challenge.

On that first day in 2005, I showed up in a black suit, pantyhose, and heels, ready to take on the world. As I walked into that tall building downtown and the window office with my name on it, I knew I'd made it. I could do anything, and I was realizing another dream. . .

. . . *A branch falling in the forest instantly transports me back into the present day.* I linger another few minutes to soak in the energy of nature all around me, before heading back to my house.

My mentor, this 21-year-old version of me, would never imagine how much clarity she's bringing me.

I sit down at my desk, open up the Florence diary, and pick up where I left off. . .

Secrets from My Travel Diaries

➢ *What you hear growing up becomes the script you follow into adulthood.*

➢ *You have the power to continue following those scripts – or not.*

➢ *Nature flows – and you can, too – when you're aligned with who you are and what you want.*

Martins Tor

Schwaben Tor

eating curry-wurst at the Markt

The beloved Bus 10

spaghetti with chopsticks?

My vineyard on Merehauserstraße

Near the University

Freiburg Bahnhof
ready to reisen...

First hell night train to
Paris...

Baquette Man in Paris

our first
Jugendharberge
in Paris

Mona Lisa in the Louvre

Museum with Napoleon's grave

The Wonderful Indian Restaurant in Paris

Whoa- the Eiffel Tower- look!

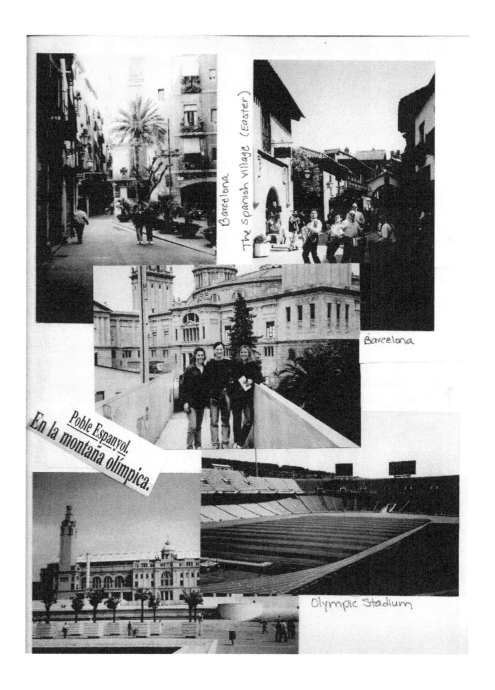

Barcelona

The Spanish village (Easter)

Barcelona

Poble Espanyol.
En la montaña olímpica.

Olympic Stadium

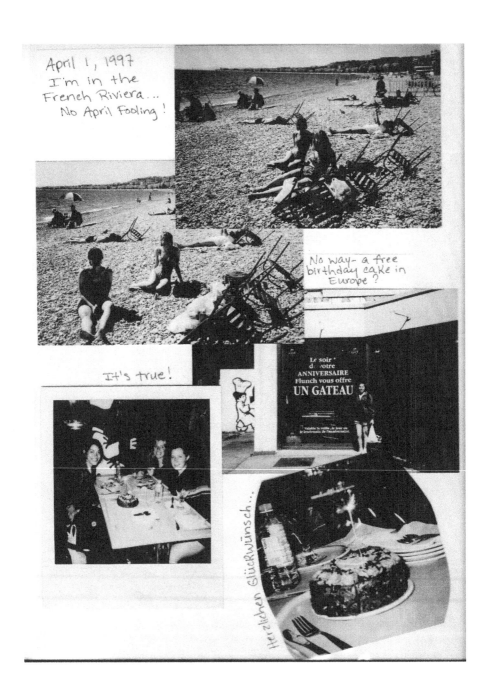

Venice – Gondola ride anyone? Na– too expensive!

The Bridge of Sighs

PART 2

ON THE JOURNEY

CHAPTER 11

Freiburg: Home Away from Home

"I feel like I was meant to be in this wonderful city, at least for now. If never again will I be this free, I just want to hold on and enjoy the ride."

April 9, 1997

I'm happy to have this beautiful, brand-new diary to write in. It has scenes of Florence on it (which is where I found it). I had been looking for a new diary because I was getting ready to run out of pages in my last one. The thought of having to conserve the remaining pages by writing less on the train ride back didn't appeal to me at all.

The other thing I'm happy about is getting my *Wildflowers* Tom Petty cassette tape back. I've been listening to it over and over because I hadn't heard it for weeks. My flatmate Felix had my tape while we were traveling, and he was gone when I got back.

A few of Tom Petty's songs have become theme songs for this time in my life. "Wildflowers" captures my feelings of wanting to be free. "Time to Move On" makes me think of all the places we have been and everything we've seen and done. "American Girl" (from the *Tom Petty and the Heartbreakers* album) makes me think about who I am: how I grew up, and who I am now – or who I am becoming.

I've been reflecting a lot lately about our travels and all that we've been doing. We met a German couple in Venice, who were traveling with a big tourist group, and the conversation with them really made me think. They were amazed that Clarissa, Anne, and I were traveling alone and looked genuinely scared for us. The conversation was short, but it made me realize two important things.

Firstly, that sweet couple need not be afraid for us. We have done just fine, coming and going as we pleased. Throughout Europe, we have found our own way on a tight budget and have done as much as most tour groups do – if not more.

We have found our own trains and hostels and food and sites. And we've done it all by ourselves, without a bus driving us around and dropping us off where they think we should go, or a tour guide leading us around. To navigate it all, we have spoken French, German, and English – a little Spanish and a little Italian. And that has led us to meet people from all over Europe, all along the way.

The other thing I've realized is how much I've missed Freiburg. Freiburg is *my* city, even though I've only been here for a short time. In Freiburg, I know how to get to most of the places I want to go. I know how to wash my clothes. I have a pillow for my bed. And here in the south of Germany, in this beautiful city, the sun shines down upon my apartment, and there are wonderful people all around me who speak a language that I speak, too.

Even despite how much I love it here, it's been difficult getting back into the swing of things, though. During our vacation, every minute of every day brought something new and exciting. I feel so "blah" now. I have some bizarre kind of culture shock, too – I guess from being back in Germany after traveling to all those other places.

This week, I took my seven rolls of film to be developed from our trip. Aside from classes, I've spent most of this week putting together my photo album. I felt a little bad about shutting myself in my room because I should be out taking advantage of every opportunity I have here. But I also know that I really needed the time to myself. It helped me snap out of whatever cloud I was in.

Honestly, I have no idea how I would remember where we've been and when, had I not started my album right away. I got most of the pages done, except for some of the captions, because I need to go back to some of the maps to figure out what we did when. Some parts of Rome looked the same to me, even when I was there. Now they *really* look the same.

Back in Freiburg, I am now finally forced to face – and resolve – my confusion about which classes to take, once and for all. I feel like the uncertainty has created some major ups and downs because I'm not used to having this many choices. Usually, my major, minors, and other requirements create my class schedule, by default.

The way classes work here is so different from in the U.S. The classes through our program are straightforward because they're built around the American system. For the ones at the university, you have to meet with the professors during their office hours to arrange to get a *Schein* [credit and a grade for the class that translates to the American system].

Class time has been endless this week. Today, I ended up getting a massive headache after sitting in class for seven and a half hours.

I'm still taking extra classes to finalize my schedule. Also, the professors are doubling up on the lecture time for the required classes this month to make up for the holidays in May. (Southern Germany has more holidays than the rest of Germany, and we'll have four-day weekends pretty much every week next month.)

My biggest question is what I should take toward my French minor. I was going to take two classes, *Hören und Sprechen* [Hearing and Speaking] and a French literature class on Marcel Proust. Now, I'm not so sure. In both classes, I'm the only American student, with the rest Germans. I'm finding it really intimidating and confusing to learn a foreign language *in* a foreign language.

In *Hören und Sprechen* I felt my confidence plummet when I saw how much better some of the people are at French than me. One of the students in my group said that she uses her French every day for work. Everyone seems to understand every word of the French dictation we write down. I never do.

I really hope I can get the tapes at the *Sprachlabor* [speaking lab], so I can practice a little bit before class next Tuesday. Otherwise, my grades could be a disaster. I already went to see the *Hören und Sprechen* professor during his one-hour-per-week office hours, to talk to him about giving me a *Schein*.

Meanwhile, I hated every minute of the French Literature class. The professor spent an endless amount of time beating one seemingly insignificant passage into the ground. Then, he proceeded to translate entire pages of Marcel Proust's work into German in a monotone for the remainder of the two hours.

The grading scale is so different here. When the time comes, I can already see that I'll have to advocate for every grade I get at the university. I'll do what I need to, though. I've worked so hard for *summa cum laude* in school; I don't want to jeopardize that.

April 12, 1997

Today we had the "Freiburg version" of Clarissa's birthday celebration with Mike, Tom, Anne, and Clarissa's *Mitbewohner* [flatmates]. Mike, Tom, Anne, and I went to the only grocery store we know of where you can find real Mexican ingredients so that we could make her favorite kind of food. We even found her favorite kind of cake mix: hazelnut!

Making the cake was a challenge. For one thing, we put in too much milk because we messed up converting milliliters to liters. So, the cake took a while to bake, and we had to turn the pan upside down and shake it to get it out.

Still, I have to say that the cake (along with the rest of the meal) tasted delicious. Later, we all boarded *Bus Zehn* [Bus 10] and went to the disco.

April 15, 1997

I find myself really enjoying my German flatmates. Earlier this week, I was shut up in my room, finishing my homework (for a class I later decided not to take), when Greta knocked on my door, inviting me for a martini.

When I emerged from my room, everyone was gathered in the living room. I joined them, and we spent hours playing a game that was like *Charades*. Each person on the team got a chance to draw, describe, or act out the words on the cards. Sometimes I needed my dictionary to find out what the word was, but I was able to play along.

I spent most of today in class and then got some things done with Clarissa. At four o'clock, we had to meet our theater class to take a bus to Stuttgart to see a play called *Andorra*. The play was very modern and interesting, especially because I could understand most of it in German. The only thing was that the theater was packed with high school groups, who whistled and laughed throughout the play, so it was hard to hear at times.

Overall, I feel like I am starting to get in the groove here. We have class Monday through Thursday, and I try to finish all the work during that time. Then, on Friday through Sunday, I can do my own thing (and maybe do a little homework here and there).

April 19, 1997

This weekend I met up with Clarissa and Anne. The day we hiked to *Saint Odile*, the couple that we walked back with told us all about *Spargel* [white asparagus] season. Apparently, it's what Freiburg is known for. So, we went to *Café Haus* and sat outside and had *Spargel* and ham wrapped in a *crepe* and covered in a decadent white sauce.

After lunch, the weather was beautiful, so we sat on a hill and made a list of the things we still want to do in Freiburg. Then we planned our next week-long trip to Austria and Hungary. We totally bonded over talk of our travels and sharing our hopes and dreams.

On Sunday afternoon, we continued our quest to see as much of Freiburg as we could while we're here. We went walking to this adorable village, lookout point, and café, where there was a wine tasting.

As we were exploring the area, we found the perfect spot in the vineyards with a beautiful panoramic view. Looking out across the horizon, I felt like singing *"The Hills Are Alive with the Sound of Music."* It was so beautiful and made me feel so free.

Clarissa said that looking back to this time in her life, she knew she would always remember the wonderful friends she'd traveled Europe with. Everything here is so new and exciting; I just want to do it all. How blissful it is to have friends who feel the same.

April 23, 1997

I've been having so much trouble concentrating on my schoolwork. It's been taking me way longer than it should to finish, because I keep daydreaming about where I want to travel and the things I want to do.

Last week I was totally stressed, to the point where I felt it in the back of my eyes, like I do when I'm at school in the U.S. Finally, this week, I've started to feel a little more relaxed. I've got to keep reminding myself not to worry so much about the things I can't control.

I guess I made an impression with the *Hören and Sprechen* professor when I met with him during his office hours. He repeatedly signaled me out as "*die Amerikanerin*" [the American] throughout his class.

At one point, he started talking about East Germany before the Reunification. He asked everyone to raise their hands if they'd been there. Only three people did (I was one since I'd been on the summer program in Lutherstadt Wittenberg in 1995).

The professor went off on a tangent about how everyone should make a point to go there. Seemingly as additional support for his argument, he kept reiterating how "*die Amerikanerin*" was among the few who'd been, too.

I guess it's not so surprising that not many have been, though. It's so different there, and reunifying a country after such a long separation takes time. Anyway, I'm looking forward to going back there to visit during *Stadtfest,* their big city festival in June.

After class, I went to the library to see if my French professor in the U.S. had responded to my email from a few days ago. I'd asked her for advice about the French literature class and whether or not I should take it. "*Marcel Proust . . . en allemand? Pas du tout!*" [Marcel Proust... in German? No way!] she'd simply written.

That was clear enough for me! I decided right then and there to stop attending the French literature class. Then, I walked back from the university, feeling like a lead weight – the heaviness of indecision – had been lifted off me.

April 24, 1997

I talked with my parents for an hour just now. When I think of growing up in small-town Ohio, I cannot believe where I live now and the life I lead. Mom told me that she would love to come visit but wouldn't feel comfortable unless I could be with her the whole way. I guess for my generation, airplanes have become nothing more than fast cars that can take you around the world. Her generation didn't grow up that way.

Talking with her reminded me of what I'm missing at home. It's not in my nature to be homesick very often; still, it's hard to miss family get-togethers and big events at school.
Sometimes, I wish I could transport myself back home for a day or two and then reappear right back into my life here. Despite occasional pangs of regret for not being at home, though, I know in my heart that right here is exactly where I need to be.

April 25, 1997

Fritz called me last night. Hearing his voice on the other end of the phone still does something to my head, though it's getting easier as time passes.

He gushed about how much my German had improved and said I'd gotten so much more confident since we last spoke. *"Es gefällt mir"* [I like it!], he said, in that way that always drives me insane. Then, he told me that Otto was planning to visit from Heidelberg this weekend, and they were wondering if we were available to go out.

I positively floated away from the phone at the end of our conversation. Reminding myself that he has a girlfriend seems to be the only thing that keeps me in check. Part of me hopes that maybe they broke up, but based on what I've seen, I doubt it.

Through Fritz, I've been learning to take the attitude that whatever happens, happens. And I'm adjusting to the notion that an invitation to go out simply means that he wants to get to know me as a friend. It by no means excludes the possibility that he may have a girlfriend.

April 27, 1997

The weather is beautiful, and I am so hoping it remains that way, as I sit here writing on a bench, soaking up the sun. There is a little spring running over the rocks, with lush greenery and flowers all around. This truly is the life!

Clarissa, Anne, and I went out with Fritz, Otto, and another friend of theirs named Faisal. Seeing them again, I felt as if I had an entirely different experience than last time. I don't know if I've improved or what, but I could totally understand Otto's German this time. It was a lot of fun going out with them, especially because we got to speak so much German, and they are genuinely nice guys.

We went to a bar with a big dance floor and lots of people. The DJ played a mixture of American dance music and German folk music. I got swept up in a kick line with a group of Germans, ended up across the dance floor from everyone, and had to dance my way back. The folk music was so much fun because all the Germans knew how to dance to it. We just did our best to follow along.

These few weeks of being in Freiburg again have been just what I needed. It feels like I've gotten so much clearer about so many things. Lately, I've realized that being here is teaching me how to deal with what life deals you. There's not much you can do about a lot of things, anyway, and I'm learning to roll with the punches. I've gotten better about that already.

I also feel that I've gained so much more understanding of who I am, kind of like seeing myself shrouded in a new light. The newness of Europe has helped me to better understand the old. I know that my light burns brighter with all that I have experienced here.

All at once, I am realizing that I'm speaking German more fluently, meeting people who stretch my thinking, and navigating a life that not long ago I couldn't even have imagined. And I'm feeling more confident about being who I am.

We went to another 21st birthday party with about 20 people from our program. I haven't been in a room with so many Americans for a long time. It was a bit overwhelming but fun. People showed up that I hadn't seen since orientation, and it was interesting to reconnect on what they've been up to while I've been living my own life on a different path.

There is still a big group from our program that regularly hangs out together. We drifted away from doing that after the first week or two, and I'm glad. Creating a "mini-America" in the middle of Europe would have made for a totally different experience. I'm thankful for being immersed in the culture here.

Next weekend restarts the crazy times of traveling all over Europe. It feels as though as soon as I settle back into my life in Freiburg, I leave again. At the same time, I can't imagine not traveling during all the holidays.

The time is now to follow my dreams – to do the things I may never do if I don't do them now. With every opportunity that comes, part of me is saying, "Go for it!" And the part of me that's still not so sure is speaking so softly now, I can barely even hear that voice anymore.

Secrets from My Travel Diaries

> ➤ *Take time for quiet reflection when you need it.*

> ➤ *Deal with what life deals you – know what you can and can't control.*

> ➤ *Confidence grows through action, and action diminishes fear.*

CHAPTER 12

Unbridled Joy
(Luzern and Interlaken, Switzerland)

"After traveling for a while, anywhere you go can start to feel like just another city. But we've had such incredibly different experiences in each place that they remain distinctive in my mind."

May 1, 1997

The craziness – and fun – of a May full of holidays has begun! Clarissa and I are on a train again, headed to Luzern, Switzerland. This is our first *Feiertag* [holiday] of the month, simply called *der erste Mai* [the 1st of May].

Yesterday we had to take an emergency trip back to the travel agency, after discovering that our reservations were for the wrong dates. We had to wait for 45 minutes to get someone to help us because the line was so long and slow. Fortunately, after all that, we got Hans as our travel agent, and he was able to fix everything for us.

Last night Anne, Clarissa, and I met up and started cooking gnocchi – just like we had in Italy. We talked for hours afterward. Then Mike, Tom, Hilda, and Mark came by and invited us to go to an all-night party. Anne isn't going to

Switzerland with us, so she went with them, but Clarissa and I still had to pack and snatch a few hours of sleep.

At five-thirty this morning, I hoisted my big backpack onto my back and headed out. I arrived at Clarissa's just as everyone else was getting home from the party. They started telling us all about it, and we ended up missing the bus.

Finally, we were able to pry ourselves away and made a mad dash down the road to catch the streetcar instead. We breathed a sigh of relief, when we made it into the streetcar. But it sat there for what seemed like an eternity, leaving us sitting helplessly inside, nervously watching the minutes tick by.

Finally, we got to the station, thinking we had missed the train. However, it was running late (which almost never happens in Germany) and didn't pull up until a few minutes later.

We hoped our luck would continue, and it did. On the train to Luzern, the fog was so thick that we were afraid we wouldn't see anything all day – let alone get any good pictures. But it lifted just as we arrived at the Luzern station, and the weather was beautiful for the rest of the day.

On top of that, our challenges with directions disappeared, once we figured out how to navigate the city. At first, we zigzagged back and forth, taking a few wrong turns. Then, we realized that as long as we knew where the river was (and which side of it we wanted to be on), we were good to go. From then on, everywhere we wanted to be, we simply stumbled upon it without even using a map.

Luzern is incredibly enchanting, with its medieval architecture and bridges. I didn't know much about the city beforehand, but Clarissa had been to Switzerland before, and her love for this picturesque country was contagious.

Switzerland was incredibly expensive, but it didn't even matter. Every moment brought unbridled joy. We ran around like school children, peeking around corners and taking photos of bridges. Something unexpectedly quaint and wonderful seemed to await us around every corner.

Right out of the train station, we stumbled upon the famous covered bridge, *Kapellbrücke mit Wasserturm* (the one in all the tourist books). Its entire story was told through paintings, all the way along the ceiling of the bridge. We walked across it, looking up, and followed it all the way.

Later, we took the funicular up for a beautiful view, and walked along the wall stretching across the city's northern part, feeling like great adventurers. We didn't spend much time in *Altstadt* [Old Town], as it was mainly just expensive shops and restaurants. Instead, we caught an afternoon boat tour (because the evening tours were way pricier).

All the dinner options exceeded our budget, so we ended up at McDonald's, which honestly was where I wanted to go, anyway. I had been craving a Swiss chocolate milkshake since we had one at a McDonald's in Geneva when I was 16. At the time, I thought it was the best shake ever. Somehow, it wasn't quite as good as I remembered, but it was still delicious.

Clarissa and I lingered over our meal at the food court long after. Our conversation flowed like a fountain, as we shared our dreams and impressions of the places we've been.

Someday, when I can afford it, I want to stay at the Hotel Château Gütsch, see Mount Pilatus, and go on a sunset boat tour with dinner and a live Alpen folk music performance. This time, though, it was enough to just be in this beautiful place. Here, we stumbled upon everything we were looking for, without a map; we were free to roam wherever we wanted, and we were fueled by nothing but unbridled joy.

After dinner, there was nothing pressing to do, and we were a little tired. It was still way too early to go out, so we went back to our hostel and took a nap. (We slept well, despite a group of loud bunkmates who sat in the room and talked the whole time.)

Later, feeling more rested, we headed to the only pub listed in the *Let's Go* book, Hotel Mr. Pickwick Pub, a British type of pub. It seemed to be the most happening place around. We sat at the bar, and I ordered something called a Lemon Hooch, which I guess is a big thing in England.

There were lots of guys in uniform, both younger and older people, and bartenders with T-shirts that said, "Where People Meet." I guess it was true, because we got to talking to a couple of people there, and they decided to teach us *Schweizerdeutsch* (Swiss German). It is different from *Hochdeutsch* (the more traditional German that we speak) and hard for us to understand.

One thing about putting yourself out there and being willing to meet people is that you learn things you never imagined. . .

May 2, 1997

Here in Interlaken, our hostel is like a world within itself. There is a grocery store, a dining room with cheap meals, and a bar. They show movies every night and provide a wealth of information on anything you might have an inkling to do.

We asked the lady at the hostel for a recommendation on what to do. She suggested a hike to Harder Kulm Mountain, so we found our way there. The trail was very steep, and we were sweating buckets in the sun, which was way hotter than we expected.

On the way up, we passed a postcard-perfect Swiss family, all four of them wearing shorts with suspenders, little hats, and socks pulled all the way up to their knees, just like in the movies. They greeted us with a spirited *"Grüezi!"* [Swiss German for "Hello"].

The whole time we were hiking up the mountain, we kept passing people going down but no one went up. Finally, we stopped to rest on a bench to eat our peanut butter and jelly sandwiches and found out why.

A couple from Brazil, who had been living in Germany for ten years, asked if they could share our bench. We got to talking with them, and they said they were surprised we hadn't taken the *funicular* up the mountain. Apparently, that was what everyone else had done!

By then, we were almost to the top and determined to finish. The trail got steeper and muddier from the springs and waterfalls. After scrambling across a grassy cliff to circumvent the pool of water on the trail, we finally reached the lookout point. We were rewarded with sweeping views of *Brienzersee* [Lake Brienz] and *Thunersee* [Lake Thun], framed by the Alps. It looked just like Switzerland in all the postcards.

The hike back down the mountain took less than half the time. On the way back, we encountered more "typical Swiss" scenery, with views straight out of every photo and guidebook.

We saw a farmhouse with cows that looked exactly like the ones on the *"La Vache Qui Rit"* [Laughing Cow] cheese label. There were a bunch of goats eating in the shade, too, and we tried to call them over to take their picture but couldn't entice them.

Without a good goat picture, but with everything else we could have ever wanted, we returned to our hostel tired and hungry. All in all, we'd hiked over five hours, mostly uphill.

We were absolutely delighted to find out that the restaurant at the hostel had *raclette* and cheese fondue. *Raclette* is a typical Swiss dish consisting of melted cheese, potatoes, pickles, and meat. It was so expensive in Luzern, but available at our hostel in Interlaken for a fraction of the price. We split the raclette and cheese fondue and enjoyed the meal immensely.

After dinner, we were going to just take a nap and a quick shower and go to a bar that was heavily recommended by *Let's Go,* because of its atmosphere and cheap beer. Instead, we both fell into a deep sleep.

Twice we tried to get up. The first time I felt like I could, but Clarissa felt like hell. The second time Clarissa was up for going, but I couldn't move a muscle. Finally, we gave up and went to sleep for the night.

May 3, 1997, 10 AM

This morning, we woke up to a five-minute shower, which turned out to be an extra charge on top of the nightly rate. The breakfast included at the hostel was a meager two pieces of bread with cheese, jam, and coffee, too.

We were all set to leave Interlaken this morning to catch a train to Zermatt and take a two-day hike up the Matterhorn. Some other backpackers planted some doubt in our minds about our plan, however. This early in the season, they warned us that we'd probably be the only hikers at the Matterhorn, and the paths are very icy. They looked worried that we might slide to our deaths with no one around to find us.

Meanwhile, there are brochures everywhere, full of things to do in Interlaken. Most of them were pretty expensive, though – hiking would be a lot cheaper. Still, it was one of the most incredibly beautiful days ever. I didn't see a cloud in the sky. This got us thinking, *Maybe the time is now.* Who knew if we'd ever have a chance like this again?

May 3, 1997, 8 PM

We decided to extend our stay in Interlaken, after all, plunking down a little over $100 to go paragliding over the Alps. The unexpected sum digs into our stash for future trips. However, the change in plans saves us a day on our Eurail passes. (We are going to take the six o'clock in the morning train to Zermatt and return to Freiburg the same day so we can still make it to class on Monday.)

On the way to our paragliding excursion, time seemed to move in slow motion, as our van climbed higher and higher up the mountain on a winding road. I felt more and more nervous about paragliding, as the van ascended.

Once we got to the top, we had to put on all this gear and listen to the instructions about how to get up in the air. It was all pretty easy because we were going tandem, and our guides were handling most of it. The guides also showed us how to take pictures, so that you could really tell that you're in the air, by making sure to get your feet in and stuff.

In our small group, we all took off one at a time. Clarissa was supposed to be first. I was terrified when she and her guide took off and then came abruptly back down a few seconds later. There ended up being a knot in her parachute that they had to stop and untangle.

Before I could panic, my guide started us running. Then, all at once, the wind caught our parachute, and we swooped up in the air. Instantly, any thoughts of fear evaporated. The feeling of it was so incredible that it is difficult to describe.

Once airborne, I had to hold onto the straps and shake myself back to sit on some kind of board. Then, I felt this incredibly peaceful, free feeling, as if I were just floating along across the breezes, with breathtaking views of the Swiss Alps surrounding me.

My guide helped me take my camera off my neck and expertly snapped a picture of us with only one hand on the camera. Then, he carefully handed it back to me, and I wrapped the camera around my wrist and took a picture with my feet framing it.

I had a moment of panic when my camera was suspended in the air, but once it was safely around my neck again, I was free to float along as I pleased. We spun around in the air, the wind currents catching us and taking us where they wanted us to go. I didn't have to worry about steering or doing anything and could just stretch out my arms and legs, totally free.

I loved every minute and wished we could have been up there for longer, swooping over the trees and lakes. All too soon, we had to start running in the air until our feet softly landed on the ground. Clarissa landed a few minutes later, and we danced and celebrated on the mountain, riding the waves of unbridled joy.

The paragliding brochure's tagline was, "Discover why the birds sing." I guess now we know. Never in my life have I felt this free!

Secrets from My Travel Diaries

- ➢ *Choose unbridled joy.*

- ➢ *Embrace and adapt to the season and your budget.*

- ➢ *Find physical and emotional freedom by releasing "should haves" and "have tos."*

CHAPTER 13

Where I Am
(The Matterhorn, Switzerland and...
Tübingen, Germany)

*"Where am I? I'm somewhere between where I was and where
I'm going, outside of which nothing else really matters."*

May 4, 1997

We arrived in Zermatt and managed to get both of our backpacks jammed into a single locker. Then, we took the cable car up to the Rippelalp stop, which the ticket vendor said had the best view for the cheapest price (that was good advice).

Those backpackers weren't kidding. When we got off the cable car, the place was deserted. There was one lonely restaurant with a sign saying it was closed until June. A nice French-speaking couple took our picture in front of the Matterhorn before taking the cable car back down.

Silence descended. We were alone.

The weather was beautiful, and the whole scene was bathed in bright sunlight amidst blue skies. The air was clear and crisp, with a slight chill because of the altitude.

Off in the distance from the other mountains, the Matterhorn stretched above the rest with its distinctive shape. It looked very majestic and a little mysterious, with a tuft of clouds shrouding its peak.

We explored the mountain with a spirit of freedom. It felt uncharted and a little eerie to be up there alone.

We came upon a makeshift bench. It was made from a single board of wood, with two rocks beneath it on either side to hold it up.

Clarissa and I sat side-by-side for a while, not saying anything, taking in the scenery and listening to the stream gurgling in the distance. It was so peaceful being in solitude with nature like that. It was as if the entire scene was made for only us.

In the distance, a tiny cabin perched on the side of the mountain captured our curiosity. Feeling like great adventurers, we hiked up to it to check it out.

Clarissa balanced on some rocks to get a view through a hole in one of the wood panels. It was deserted and looked like a storage place of some kind. It amazed us how perfectly framed you could see the Matterhorn through the hole.

We attempted to capture the view by taking a picture through the hole. (It will be interesting to see how that photo comes out when we develop the film.) Then, we climbed over the dip in the mountain and through a snowbank until we got to a terrace that looked out over the valley.

Feeling like we were on top of the world was awe-inspiring. We tried to make our voices echo over the valley, but nothing came back to us. Together in unison, we broke instead into a rendition of "Edelweiss." It seemed the perfect "typical" song to accompany the view of the Matterhorn and the Swiss Alps.

As we headed back down, our carefree bliss was shattered when an avalanche of snow suddenly crashed over the rocks right across from us. At first, it looked and sounded like a waterfall, but it was pure snow.

We were out of the danger zone of the falling snow that buried the surroundings below. Still, we were struck by the power of that avalanche, which instantly shattered the peaceful silence. What a small chance a mountain climber would have against such forces! I can understand why the mountain has become the legend that it has.

The avalanche shifted the carefree vibe of the day. As we headed back in the late afternoon sun, the Matterhorn looked different than it had before. Now, it appeared more foreboding than majestic, a place of incredible beauty but also a force that commanded respect.

We rode the cable car back down and warmed up at *Cafe Du Pont*, the oldest cafe in Zermatt. Inside, they were toasting delicious *raclette* over a cozy oven. We ordered our final *raclette* of the trip – with two huge slabs of cheese toasted over bread, surrounded with pickles, onions, and potatoes.

As we filled up from the warm, cozy food, we talked about the avalanche and the forces of nature we had witnessed. We felt so free, and everything seemed to go our way. But the force of the avalanche reminded me that the feelings of being in control can crumble in the fragility of a single moment.

Being in control is ultimately just an illusion…

May 7, 1997

It's midterms already. Fortunately, I managed to complete my theater assignment and turn it in before leaving again for another holiday weekend. (This thing about having to take classes sure is a pain.)

After class, Clarissa and I went to reserve our train tickets to *Rothenburg ob der Tauber,* the medieval walled city of Germany. We decided we were going to make a side trip there before meeting Anne in Salzburg, Austria, the next day.

Our schedule was tight because we didn't want to miss classes, so we couldn't leave until the afternoon. We met in front of the *Mensa,* left directly for the train station, and took four different trains in the space of three hours to get there.

As we approached our final stop on the train, I caught a glimpse of a wall and assumed it was part of the walled city. Clarissa had her doubts, though, because it didn't look at all like the picture.

We got off the train and asked the ticket salesman for a map. There were no free tourist maps, which seemed strange for one of the top tourist attractions in Germany. Nevertheless, we chipped in for a map and sat on a bench to look at it and get our bearings. I was certain that once we figured out where we were, we would be in for an amazing experience.

But something wasn't right.

The map we'd bought said, *"Rottenburg."*

But the place we'd wanted to go to was *"Rothenburg."*

The cities were just one letter off (and one letter off was one letter too many).

A look at the index in *Let's Go* confirmed the error. The maze of four trains that we'd been on had taken us to *Rottenburg am Neckar.* We were on the Neckar River, not the Tauber. The disgruntled travel agent we'd dealt with instead of Hans had sent us to the wrong city!

I was freaking out. Where were we? And how in the world could we get to *Rothenburg ob der Tauber?*

We went back to the shop to return the map and figure out how to get to the other *Rothenburg*. When we tried to take it back, at first the ticket guy would not let us. Finally, he relented that we could have something else in exchange. So we ordered two ice cream cones for the same price as that stupid map.

Then, we went to the ticket booth and asked how to get to *Rothenburg ob der Tauber*. No trains were going there anymore, though, as it was already late afternoon.

Back on our bench, we debated what to do. There was no way of communicating a change of plans to Anne. One way or another, we had to be at the train station in Salzburg when she showed up the next morning. It looked like we were stuck in the wrong *Rottenburg* until we could pick up the night train.

I railed against the travel agent. Why would she send two American tourists to this town? Wouldn't she know that we wanted to go to *Rothenburg*, not *Rottenburg*? And how could we have known that there were two cities with (almost) identical names?

There was that control thing again – that lesson I'd learned at the Matterhorn. I realized how little control we really had over our itinerary. That travel agent had the power to transport us wherever she wanted. Hopefully, there weren't two Salzburgs, too.

We consulted *Let's Go* to see how we could salvage the situation. Maybe there was something to see in this town, after all, or perhaps somewhere nearby.

Tübingen. That town looked kind of interesting. It was a 10-minute train ride away and had a unique-looking courthouse and a 500-year-old university. A train to Tübingen was about to leave, so we hopped aboard.

When we arrived in Tübingen, there was no tourist map there, either, but there was a map of the city painted on a wall. We decided to follow along near the river and see some of the places we'd read about in *Let's Go*.

In front of the courthouse, Clarissa made a waving motion as I took her picture. "Here I am in Tübingen, for some reason, and soon I'll be leaving again," she announced, posing for the picture.

The "Tübingen wave" had been invented. By this time, as annoyed as I was, I had to admit the whole ridiculous situation was beginning to seem a little funny.

After our brief sightseeing tour, we sat on a bench overlooking the river, looking out at Tübingen as we ate the sandwiches we'd packed. Then, we circled back to the train station and ended up back at the pub we'd seen on the way.

We had long since decided we needed to make a toast to the messed-up way we'd gotten to Tübingen. So, for the next couple of hours until our next train, we talked and laughed over a *Hefeweizen* [German beer, *Hefe* means "yeast" and *Weizen* translates to "wheat."] at the pub, periodically injecting a Tübingen wave into the conversation.

It was a very strange experience to realize that we hadn't the slightest clue where in Germany we were, but it turned out to be pretty fun.

Connecting back through the wrong *Rottenburg* and the continuation of our itinerary, we were not yet done suffering through the travel agent's handiwork. We had a very bad connection and got stranded in Plochingen (wherever that is) around midnight, for about an hour. Gone were the throngs of tourists we usually encountered en route. It was deserted, cold, and creepy.

We took shelter in the elevator – the only protected place. Huddled together with our big backpacks on, we munched on some pretzels. We were just starting to relax when a couple of creepy guys appeared and started pushing buttons, leering at us through the glass. They made the elevator come back up to them a couple of times as we kept pushing the button down to get away. Finally, the door opened on another floor, and we darted out, terrified.

We found a bench and waited in the cold near a smattering of other passengers. It was very eerie to see the trains rushing by at night. They streaked across the tracks, shrieking through the darkness. Somehow, like the Matterhorn that had turned from majestic to foreboding, the friendly trains that had signified adventure now seemed frightening and intimidating.

Sparks flew across the tracks as the trains roared past us. The minutes crawled by. Finally, a beacon of light appeared from a distance. It got larger and brighter as our train slowed to a stop at last.

We boarded the train with relief and slept most of the way to Salzburg, even without a *couchette*. That train car had become our sanctuary.

Secrets from My Travel Diaries

➢ *What you see depends on the lens through which you see it.*

➢ *Not everything will go the way you want it to – but it's here to teach you something.*

➢ *Control is an illusion.*

CHAPTER 14

Not What We Thought
(Salzburg, Austria and Munich, Germany)

"These past few days have not been what I thought
they'd be, but they've still been fun."

May 8, 1997

When we staggered off the train at five o'clock in the morning, seeing Anne waiting for us was a huge relief. (At least that dumb lady hadn't screwed that up, too.)

Our circumstances were still not great, though. At that hour, there was absolutely nothing open, nowhere to sit, and no hostel to go to. (The one we'd booked was shut tight for another two hours.)

There was nothing to do but stand and wait, heavy backpack straps digging into our shoulders, for the next hour and a half. We huddled together, chatting and munching on snacks. It was cold and awful.

Even though it was already May, it felt colder than that day we froze our butts off in Holland at the end of March. My small room with the bright white walls and cozy bed in Freiburg felt light years away.

At last, daylight transformed the darkness and put us more at ease. When the clock crawled to six-thirty in the morning, we headed over to our hostel. Shops were beginning to open, and people were walking through the streets, a sea of black umbrellas in the chilly, drizzling rain.

We waited for what seemed like an eternity outside the hostel, standing in the rain. Our room wasn't ready when we were finally able to check in, but at least we were able to leave our bags. Cold and hungry, we wandered around in the drizzle, trying to find a McDonald's. We never saw one and finally turned back.

It was a good day for a bus tour. There was just enough time to check into our room and eat one of the peanut butter and jelly sandwiches we'd brought. Then, we went outside the hostel to catch our *Sound of Music* tour.

Our tour guide was this fun Scottish guy who had lived all over the world and spoke four or five languages. His enthusiasm carried through the cold, wet rain, which persisted for nearly the entire day.

We stopped at several of the places where the movie was filmed – the gazebo where Maria and the Baron danced, the church, the von Trapp home, and the hill where Maria sings "The Hills Are Alive."

The last stop was in a small, nearby town, where the *Sound of Music* filmmakers had used the inside of the church for Maria's wedding scene. We took turns walking in Maria's steps down the aisle of the church, imagining the long train of her wedding dress flowing behind us.

At the end of the tour, we found a quaint, cozy café. We ordered goulash soup and cake, feeling like we'd stepped into heaven.

On our own after the tour, we continued to *Mirabellgarten*, also in *The Sound of Music*. Then we went to Mozart's *Geburtshaus* [Birthplace], where we saw his belongings, manuscripts, and the instruments he played.

We were drenched and annoyed at that point, so we went to another café and had coffee. When we came out, it was not raining, which only lasted for about an hour but was a total blessing. We spent the brief reprieve playing with the giant chess board at *Kapitelplatz* [Chapter Square], and visiting Saint Peter's *Friedhof*, where the cemetery was replicated for the movie set.

Despite the shaky beginnings and the incessant rain, we felt like we had salvaged the day.

May 9, 1997

Clarissa and I are heading to *München* [Munich] to meet Anne, Mike, and Tom. Anne will turn 21 at midnight tonight, so there will be a lot to celebrate.

Anne went ahead on her own, but Clarissa and I decided to stop through Füssen to see *Neuschwanstein* and *Hohenschwangau* Castle. We walked around Füssen and saw some people wearing lederhosen.

It was incredibly exciting to be in Bavaria, where the typical dress, dialect, and overall atmosphere are so different from any other part of Germany. There were Biergartens and typical Bavarian music playing everywhere. We ate *Weisswurst* [veal sausages], a typical food, and soaked in the atmosphere.

We took guided tours through both *Neuschwanstein* and *Hohenschwangau*. Again, we were the only ones walking up there, as everyone else took the minibus from Füssen. We didn't mind, though. That walk was nothing compared to the beast we'd climbed in Switzerland a week ago.

The view of the fountains around *Hohenschwangau* caught my eye, and I tried twice to capture a good picture from different angles. I didn't like the view from the lens either time, so I never ended up taking the picture, though.

We found a field by one of the castles, and Clarissa took a picture of me in the *Wildflowers*, which was consistent with the theme. . .

May 11, 1997

This trip hasn't worked out as well as the others, but in the end, we had a great time, and everything was good. The one thing that really didn't work out was Anne's birthday.

When we arrived at our hostel in Munich around eight o'clock at night, we expected to find Anne, Mike, and Tom waiting to go out. However, we found Anne sick in bed instead. We ended up having to go out to a Biergarten without her.

Our hostel in Munich was atrociously expensive – especially considering I had to sleep in a random room with people I didn't know, away from Clarissa and Anne. Also, there was only one shower, and we had to wait 45 minutes for it. Then, to top it off, they ran out of bread at the breakfast they had charged us an extra 5 deutsche marks for.

Anne tried to go sightseeing with us on her birthday but felt awful. She made it through *Schloss Nymphenburg* [Nymphenburg Palace], but when we got to the botanical gardens, we ended up having to leave her on a bench while we went in. After going to visit Saint Peter's Church and climbing up for a panoramic view of the city, she decided she couldn't take it anymore and went back to the hotel to sleep.

Regretfully, we had to leave Anne in the hotel the night of her 21st birthday. We gave her a *Bayerische* teddy bear and a card and headed to the *Hofbräuhaus,* feeling so sad, but there was nothing we could do except let her sleep.

At the *Hofbräuhaus,* all the staff were dressed in traditional attire. Our waitress was wearing lederhosen and a white dress with frills. We ordered giant pretzels and liters of beer in the famous *Steine* [mugs]. That was followed by *Würstchen* [sausage], with both the regular and more typical sweet mustard, and the best potato salad ever.

Clarissa and I ate both until we felt so full we could barely move. Clarissa couldn't even finish her last sip of beer and had to leave it sitting there in the glass.

After that, we went to a place that had advertised a *Bayerische Abend* [Bavarian evening] for 8 deutsche marks. It was too late to get a reservation, so they told us to just show up, and they'd be able to get us in.

We showed up early, found a seat where there was a band already playing, and ordered another liter of beer to share between us. When we asked the waiter, we realized that the *Bayerische Abend* was upstairs and that we couldn't bring our beer with us. To ensure a spot at the *Bayerische Abend,* we had no choice but to gulp down the liter of beer and head out quickly. Needless to say, we were a bit *beschwipst* [buzzed] when we went up to get our tickets.

The ticket seller told us she was assigning us to a "multinational table." This meant that our table was occupied by people from Sweden, Germany (Hamburg), and Switzerland; the entire rest of the room was occupied by a large tourist group from Japan.

We had to meet the minimum order, so we ordered another beer and another pretzel to split between us. Barely able to hold another swallow, we got Anne the sweatshirt she wanted, chatted with the couples from our table, and waited for the music to begin.

It was an awesome night of "*prost*"-ing [German for "Cheers"] and swaying and trying to sing traditional songs. We especially enjoyed the man from

Hamburg. He talked with us a lot and seemed to really get a kick out of us. At one point, he turned on his video recorder, panned it over to us, and narrated "American girls" into it with his thick German accent, which cracked us up.

Our whole table really got into the music. Throughout the night, people from other tables came over to take pictures of us linking arms, swaying, and singing – perhaps never suspecting how few of us were actually German. When the band played *Edelweiss,* Clarissa and I danced and sang together, and the staff called us up to dance in front of the band.

It was surreal, starting the night gulping a liter of beer to avoid being shut out of the *Bayerische Abend,* and ending it doing our own kind of waltz to *Edelweiss,* amidst video narration by people from all over the world.

Now I'm at last caught up on writing, and we are heading back to Freiburg on the train. Anne is finally feeling better. Perhaps being sick is simply a rite of passage, as all three of us have been sick at different times and have had to take care of one another. I guess if Anne had never gotten sick, she wouldn't have been properly inaugurated.

As I stop to reflect on these past several days, it feels like some of the places we've been are beginning to blend together now. I guess there are stages to traveling, and we have hit a new level.

Spending days on end looking at old churches just doesn't do it for us anymore. It's the people we've met who have taught us about the culture – and made our experience what it is.

It's hard to believe it was only days ago that we were on the train to the wrong *Rottenburg.* Now, after all we've been through, finding the places we want to go is starting to get easier. Overcoming all the little things that go wrong doesn't seem so difficult anymore, either.

Above all, what really makes the difference – especially when you're sick or tired or just really frustrated – is to know you have your friends by your side. Clarissa really stepped up to turn our situation around on this trip when I was too tired to do it. I've had my time to do that, too, and so has Anne. That's what it means to travel with people you can count on.

More and more, we're finding ourselves feeling more comfortable traveling. In fact, lately, we've been playing travel agents for other travelers. So many people did that for us in the beginning, and now we're doing that, too.

I feel like I'm developing a different perspective on what really matters, too. I doubt we'll have time to make another run at getting to *Rothenburg ob der Tauber* (It's not the only place we're missing because it's either too expensive or we just don't have time to go). There was a time when that would have really bothered me, but disgruntled travel agents and all, somehow, I've let it all go.

Secrets from My Travel Diaries

> ➢ *Even if your day doesn't turn out as expected, it can be unexpectedly fun (unless you're sick!).*

> ➢ *The people you meet make travel (and life!) what it is.*

> ➢ *Check that you're in the right place before you order.*

CHAPTER 15

Problem-Solving
(Innsbruck and Vienna, Austria)

"On the train to Vienna, we got into conversation with a nice German man and his daughter. The man said he'd been on that same train a week ago, and saw two other Americans writing in their diaries, too."

May 15, 1997

We had to return to Freiburg for midterms and spent the past few days cramming until two o'clock in the morning. It felt like total regurgitation, filling out the answers on the tests. Now, we're headed to Austria: Innsbruck and Vienna.

Our original plan was to leave this morning, but we didn't find out about today's midterm until earlier this week. We had to rework our plans, to catch a late afternoon train instead. We had the option to connect in either Stuttgart or Basel. We picked Stuttgart because it would get us into Innsbruck at midnight, instead of two o'clock in the morning.

Needless to say, after all those midterms, we were ready to get the hell out of Freiburg. However, we soon realized we hadn't remembered to bring the paper with the information about the *pension* [European version of a bed &

breakfast] we were staying in. (We'd gotten the name from one of the students in our program, so we had no way of knowing how to find the place and didn't remember the name.)

We got that problem taken care of by finding a phone booth in the train station and calling Clarissa's place. Hilda answered right away, found the piece of paper where Clarissa described it, and read it to us over the phone.

Things went all right until we got to Munich – a complete retracing of our steps from just days ago because of midterms. Then, the next problem that arose was that our train never came. It turned out that I had been looking at the summer train schedule instead. There wasn't another one for another hour and a half.

Clarissa found another payphone and called the *pension* in Innsbruck. The lady told us that she had already given our room away because we had already arrived too late (even though we'd told her what time we would get in). She then became irate and said that we would have to wait on the porch until eight o'clock in the morning when a room would be free.

I was impressed by how Clarissa stepped up, speaking firmly to the woman in confident German. At this point, we've learned that if we don't stand up for ourselves, no one else will. Finally, the lady told Clarissa to call back in 10 minutes. When she did, she had miraculously found a bed for each of us – thank goodness.

The next problem was that our Eurail passes weren't good after midnight, and the train had us arriving in Innsbruck at one-thirty in the morning. We bought supplemental tickets, which only cost 15 deutsche marks ($9). This seemed unbelievably cheap, so we hoped it was true.

Now, we are sitting at the same Burger King we were at just days ago on our trip to Munich. That feels like an eternity ago. This is probably the lowest point I've ever had in Freiburg or in all our travels. It can only get better from here.

May 17, 1997

Before things got better, they got a good deal worse, unfortunately. We got on the train at almost midnight. The train was bound for Florence, and it was as packed as the Plochingen station had been empty.

We got on with a huge group of German-speaking high schoolers who were trying to find seats, too. They kept pushing past us in a sea of people. The group leader kept asking at every compartment if there were any seats free (which there weren't), and yelling for them to keep going.

Not sure what else to do, we finally sat down on the floor, in the only tiny, empty space we could find. Unfortunately, it was right next to the bathroom, so we kept getting stepped on and stepped over by people going in and out. Finally, we noticed some pull-down aisle seats and sat there.

I heard Clarissa chatting with a guy who said he was from Mexico. He didn't have a reserved seat, either (he was stuck without one all the way to Florence!). The sound of their voices filtered in through my sleep as I dozed off, leaning against the wall with my trusty fleece as a pillow again.

When we finally arrived, we took a cab to the guest house. We simply followed the recommendation, and didn't check the hostel's location when we booked it. It turned out to be all the way up a mountain in a little village outside of Innsbruck, called Mutters.

When we arrived, the lady was waiting for us, as nice as could be. We felt bad we'd made her wait up for us, but there wasn't much we could do. Grateful just to have a bed, we didn't even know how to thank her.

The next morning, there turned out to be only one shower for everyone staying there. We waited in line, only to find that the drain was clogged and the water was freezing. After the shower from hell, things got better, as the lady made us feel at home, serving us coffee and bread and jam for breakfast and making a fuss over us.

The long breakfast table was filled with English-speaking people who didn't speak German. As she served the breakfast, she started off speaking to Clarissa and me in English, and then she would stop herself and say, *"Sie sprechen ja Deutsch"* ["They speak German"] and switch to German. She got so excited that we spoke German that after a while, she spoke only in German and asked us to translate for the other guests.

It was a beautiful day and the first time I've worn shorts since I've been here. We followed the tourist map all around Innsbruck, but a lot of the day was a blur.

We went up the *Stadtturm [Town Tower]* for the panoramic view, then to the *Alpenzoo.* After lunch, we felt so tired, we were convinced that we would not be able to get up again, but somehow we did.

The other place we wanted to visit was the Olympic Stadium. It took a while to get there because we had to take a bus and *Straßenbahn* [street car], but we figured it out.

We returned to the city, determined to find the places on the map that we couldn't find earlier in the day. Only then did we realize that we had been past all those places at least three times already but had been so tired we hadn't realized.

At the end of the day, we took the *Straßenbahn* back to our hotel, getting off one stop too soon and having to walk the rest of the way.

Overall, we enjoyed the *pension* experience. It was the first time we'd been in a real home in a long time, which was such a wonderful feeling. Despite the rocky start, the lady who ran the *pension* was so kind to us and really made us feel at home. Being there kind of reminded me of the times my cousins and I stayed at our grandparents' house on weeklong vacations growing up.

The only thing that wasn't so good about staying there was that we kept screwing up the protocols she had in place. Our major screw-up was, of course, keeping her up until two o'clock in the morning. In addition to that, she had to tell us three times not to close the door so loudly, and we somehow lost one of the tokens for the shower. We messed up another time when we sat across from each other at breakfast instead of next to each other.

After our one whirlwind day in Innsbruck, we left for Vienna after breakfast, taking a train and a ferry to *Chiemsee* [the Bavarian Sea] on the way. There wasn't much going on in *Chiemsee,* though it was very beautiful.

We took a German tour of the *Königsschloß*, which looks similar to Versailles in Paris. According to the tour guide, it was built as a sort of competition between King Ludwig II in Germany and King Louis XIV in France).

We wandered around after that and ended up in a field with a bunch of cows. An American guy was walking by, and we asked him if there was anything else to do there. He said he didn't think so. Then, a German-speaking guy walked by and asked us the same thing, to which we gave him the same answer.

After taking a nice nap on a lawn by a church, we went to get our stuff out of our locker to leave for Vienna. However, the top part of the locker key was broken off, and we couldn't get the door open. We asked the kiosk worker, who instructed us to go to another guy.

The guy growled at us and kept insisting we must have the wrong locker. He even asked if we were certain we had left our bags there and not at some other train station. Finally, he jiggled the key around a couple of times, and it came open, much to our relief.

May 19, 1997

Clarissa and I are relaxing by the Danube River, catching up on our diaries so we don't forget everything by our next train ride. We are staying in Vienna and Budapest longer this time, so it is more difficult to keep up.

Like in Innsbruck, we are staying at a family-run *pension* here in Vienna. At least this time, we arrived at ten forty-five at night instead of one o'clock in the morning. Clarissa had been in charge of those reservations, too, and when we arrived and she called our hotel, the woman replied happily, "You are Clarissa!"

We took the *Straßenbahn* to the *pension* and had to *schwarzfahren* [ride without paying], because we didn't know how to work the ticket machine. *Schwarzfahren* makes me very nervous, but fortunately, we didn't get caught, and we didn't know what else to do.

The husband, who looked about 80 years old, was there waiting for us when we got out of the *Straßenbahn*. As we walked the couple of blocks to our hostel, he kept repeating in English, "My wife is explaining everything in the morning."

When we got to the pension, the poor man couldn't find the keys, so his wife had to get out of bed and open the door for us. We felt bad, but she brushed it off, saying it was a "nice midnight stroll."

The next morning, she served us breakfast in our room and gave us a map and a detailed explanation of what to do and where to go. The breakfast was wonderful: meat, cheese, jelly, rolls, bread, coffee, and tea. It cost an extra $5, but it was worth it. It felt nice to be pampered a little.

We took the subway to the *Innere Stadt* [1st District, Vienna's Old Town]. Outside the opera house, we were immediately accosted by people dressed up in old-fashioned costumes, pushing some Mozart show. (This happened about five more times that day.)

Because it was Sunday, the museums were free, including the headset, which provided all kinds of information. At the antique instrument museum in the National Library, it was fascinating seeing the instruments that have been playing throughout history.

I hadn't realized that Ben Franklin had invented an instrument called the glass armonica, which Mozart later learned to play. It turns out Mozart played for Napoleon and Maria Antoinette, too. I had never thought about them all living at the same time and knowing each other.

The other thing we did was to go to *Praterstern*, the park with the Ferris wheel. We paid $5 to go on it, and it provided a beautiful view. However, for some reason, it didn't even go around a full time – the operators just kept loading and unloading people, and when it came around again, you had to get off. It was neat but kind of a rip-off.

In the afternoon, we'd arranged with Tom before we left Freiburg that we'd meet him in front of the opera house at two o'clock. He was supposed to be traveling to Vienna with visitors from the U.S. For some reason, he never showed up (hopefully he's okay!). We had to go to the *Original Sachertorte* without him. (The *Sachertorte,* in our opinion, was good but high-priced.)

The biggest thing we noticed about Vienna was that everywhere we went, from on the street to in the opera house, somebody seemed to be making beautiful music somewhere. Our opera house experience was the ultimate. Two hours before the opera was to begin, we got in line for one of the 160 *Stehplätze* [standing places] available.

It was not all that comfortable standing up for the two-hour production of the *Philharmoniker*, but I guess the production is a really big thing. Standing was worth it to be able to go for only $2 a ticket.

I felt completely gripped by the music, even standing in the back in the stuffy heat. The opera was generally instrumental, with one woman singing during about the last half hour. The opera house itself was phenomenal, too, with awesome acoustics and a deep red décor. It was like nothing I'd ever seen before.

After the *Philharmoniker* – just when we thought we were doing well with directions – we realized we'd lost our map somewhere. We somehow got all turned around finding our way back from the subway. After asking a few people for directions with no luck, we happened to run into our classmate from our program (the one who would recommend the *pension* to us in the first place!), and walked back with her.

It's time to leave Vienna. Everything seems so expensive here. It will be nice to go next to Budapest, where we will feel like we can afford more things. *Bis später…* [Until later…]

Secrets from My Travel Diaries

➢ *When the unexpected happens, solve one problem at a time.*

➢ *Stand up for yourself, or no one else will.*

➢ *When in Vienna, go to the opera, even if you have to stand up the whole time.*

CHAPTER 16

To the Unknown Again (Budapest)

"We were talking about how many places we've been since our plane landed in Frankfurt and were wondering how much distance we've actually traveled. It would definitely be interesting to find out."

May 20, 1997, 10 AM

There is nothing more nerve-racking than being en route to somewhere, in total angst about what awaits you at the end of the line. I feel kind of like I did on the plane to Frankfurt a few months ago. Part of me doesn't want to arrive where we are going; another part of me is incredibly curious about what lies ahead.

I'm really nervous about going to Hungary, even though it was one of the places I most wanted to go when we were dreaming about it at school. It is part of my heritage. As a kid, I heard stories about my great-grandmother migrating from Hungary to the U.S. as a teenager. Even though I was young when she passed away, the long lines of apple strudel that would stretch across her kitchen table are still etched in my mind.

I've never felt, in all our travels, quite like I do right now, riding this train through Hungary. When we looked at the map, we realized how much further east we are than we've ever been in our lives. I feel like I'm crossing a border that most Americans don't cross.

Two stern-looking men came by to check our passports. Uniformed guards keep walking up and down the aisles. It feels like we're entering a different world. This country is so different from anywhere else we've been. Communist times were not so long ago here.

It really freaked me out when we ran into friends last night, and they warned us about going. We know other people who have gone there and been fine, though. I think that as long as we are careful, we will be okay.

Still, I do not like the fact that we are arriving in the dark. It also freaks me out that we couldn't change any Hungarian money in advance because the banks don't carry any due to inflationary problems. When we arrive, we will have no Hungarian money and no idea where our hotel is.

May 21, 1997, 2 PM

We are traveling on a squeaky train across miles of farmland. The houses we've been passing are gray and rundown, but the people seem to dress the same as they would anywhere else.

For the first time in our travels, I feel like I don't fit in. Being different is one thing, but feeling completely out of place is quite another. I'm interested to see what happens next.

May 21, 1997, 11 PM

Clarissa and I somehow survived the ordeal of getting here and are now safely in our hostel. The hostel we originally booked made me a little nervous because we knew nothing about it. I guess there have been a lot of problems with people being taken for all they're worth there. We have definitely heard some horror stories, but I think it will be alright if we watch each other's backs.

This hostel is a dump and costs a mere $5 per night. It is part of the Hostel International network, though, which makes me feel better.

When we got off the train in Budapest, it was as if we'd stepped into a different time period. The train station was sketchy. People everywhere were offering us rooms for much more money than we could afford.

We waded through the swarm and ran into an American man, on a layover to Istanbul. He looked about middle-aged and said he had been all over the world. He fed us one horror story after another about getting robbed, but finally helped us out by directing us to the lady at the tourist office.

She was nice and helpful, instructed us where to go, and gave us directions and a map. We also raised our concerns about not having any local currency, and she assured us that we didn't have to pay for the bus and could pay for the hostel tomorrow.

Once we got outside the train station, despite her directions, we got confused all over again about where to go. As we stood there, not knowing what to do, we ran into the American man again. He told us he had nothing to do for an hour until his next train, then started launching into more nerve-racking stories. It was dark and scary, and this was only making matters worse.

Just as we were searching for an exit plan, the lady from the tourist office appeared. She was heading home at the end of her shift and offered to walk with us to the bus stop.

After she left, we spent a tense 5-10 minutes in a sketchy area, waiting for the bus. When it finally came, the only seats available were facing backward. We squeezed onto the mini-bus with our big backpacks and sat in the backward seats, feeling conspicuous as if under a spotlight.

Everyone on the bus sat in silence, expressionless. The bus sputtered through the darkness for what seemed like forever. Fortunately, the travel agent's directions were good. We kept our eyes peeled for the hostel, and with its big sign lit up in the darkness, we found it with no problem.

I've never been so happy to see the inside of a hostel in my life. It's called the Party Hostel because of the loud 24-hour bar downstairs, but right now, I'm just glad to have a bed. It seems safe, and I feel like we can trust that they will charge what they said they will. Right now, that is more than sufficient.

May 24, 1997

On our first day in Budapest, we woke up early in our pit of a hostel and got out of there as quickly as we could. It took a while to figure out how to change money. When we went to McDonald's afterward, people looked at us like we were insane when we pronounced the words on the screen, but we managed to order.

Everywhere we went, we felt people looking at us. It was the first time I really felt like I was somewhere I didn't belong. Some people stared and whispered, seeming to openly despise us. Others looked at us with curiosity. When they did, I couldn't help but look back at them in fascination.

I'm thinking that when it comes down to it, people are people everywhere you go. It is their environment that changes them. In Budapest, the people looked and dressed virtually the same as we did, but something about them was different. They seemed like they had been through a lot.

We met fewer Americans in Budapest than anywhere else we've traveled. I guess most are much more apt to go to Western Europe.

The other Americans we did meet told us that they were only touring Eastern Europe and skipping Western Europe altogether. They said they felt like Eastern Europe would change and Western Europe wouldn't as much, so they wanted to see it while they were young and able to deal with the infrastructure and the challenges. I'm glad we did what we did, but I agree that Eastern Europe is something to be experienced.

We headed to the castle district first. On the way there, we stumbled upon the Parliament building across the river in Pest. It was one of the most amazing places I have ever seen. The castle district and the royal palace blew my mind, too.

On the way to Margaret Island, the weather was beautiful but also windy. Both my only scrunchie and Clarissa's camera case blew away. I never did find another good scrunchie, but Clarissa bought a nice camera case for about $5 from one of the street vendors.

We really wanted to try some Hungarian cuisine, and looked around for the restaurant *Let's Go* recommended. The road wasn't where it was supposed to be, according to the map, though. For some reason, a lot of the streets we passed weren't on the map, either.

We walked around forever, asking at one McDonald's and then another. They were very helpful but didn't know exactly where it was. Finally, we went into a Burger King, and someone there knew.

Frustrated and starved, we finally found the place and ordered chicken paprikash with fries and Hungarian beer. They had something like 100 kinds of beers available. The waiter was young and good-looking and explained the menu to us in English.

We stayed a while at the restaurant, enjoying the delicious food and people-watching. It has been very difficult to talk to anyone here. We feel so incredibly different we don't even know how to begin. It has been very difficult to communicate, too. Most people don't speak English, though some, mainly in the older generation, speak German.

Wandering through the streets of Budapest the following day, we found a place called The New York Bagel Restaurant. Not having eaten bagels in an eternity, we went there three days in a row. We ordered bagels, muffins, and a cappuccino for under $2, seeing probably every American in the city there.

After that, we went to the city park, where we happened into the *Széchenyi Baths*, thinking we were going into a castle. We decided to enter the baths but had major problems communicating with the attendant. Finally, someone walking by spoke to us in German and helped translate.

We were given a towel and an apron-like thing to wear, which was about the size of a napkin and exposed most of our front and entire backside. Once we worked up the courage to go out there, the baths felt positively wonderful, and it wasn't so bad being naked, as the place was nearly empty.

Everywhere we went around the city, as long as we could get there on the metro, finding it was easy and efficient. We rode everywhere on our three-day pass for only $6.

When we had to travel by bus, though, it was a different situation entirely. There were no signs to label the stops, so we never knew when to get off. Sometimes we had to ride until the end and go back the other way, once we figured out where we wanted to be.

One day we were looking for the right bus to the Pál-völgyi Cave (apparently, Budapest is the only city in the world with a cave so close by). We ended up asking some guy walking by. He told us that he had only a *"kleines Verständnis"* [basic understanding] of German, but he ended up knowing enough German to help us find the bus, which took us right there.

All the food we had in Hungary was delicious, and there were wonderful smells everywhere. Even the metro was filled with the most delicious aromas from the underground bakery. The vanilla pastries that were positively wonderful.

That evening, we went out to eat at a restaurant I picked specifically because it was easy to find from a metro stop. We ordered goulash soup and this peach juice that I wish we had in America. For our main course, we ordered pork with dumplings, which is a traditional dish according to *Let's Go.* There was this white sauce with paprika on top of the entire thing, which was so delicious.

We left the restaurant so stuffed that we could barely move (typical for our time in Budapest). After checking out the views of the city at night, we went back to "The Dump" (our nickname for our hostel). When I tried to crawl into my bunk, there was someone sleeping in my bed, and I had to go back to the desk to be assigned another one.

On our last day, we took the bus to the nearby town of *Szentendre.* We checked our bags at the train station's luggage room, thinking we could do the day excursion and leave directly from there.

Szentendre is a beautiful town with the neatest-looking roofs I've ever seen and windy streets with cobblestones. It is apparently the most touristic city in Hungary besides Budapest, so most of the souvenirs were very expensive. However, we were able to find some affordable ones in a series of shops away from the main drag.

Next, we hopped on another train, this time to Esztergom, on the border of Slovakia. When we stopped for goulash soup and some wonderful ice cream, the waiter told us that we could hop a boat across the lake to get to Slovakia. We decided to do it, just to set foot in yet another country.

The boat was barely seaworthy but only cost 90 forints (less than $1, I think). When we got near the shore, all we could see was a faded sign that said "Slovakia," with five intimidating-looking armed guards in uniform standing in front of it.

At that point, the driver informed us that this was the last boat back to Hungary. We started to flip out about getting stuck there and not making it back to Freiburg. So, we ended up bargaining with the Slovakian boat driver in German to take us back to Hungary for another 90 forints.

He agreed and also gave us a minute to go ashore to Slovakia and take a picture of the sign. We stepped onto land without crossing over past the guards, took the picture, and then got back in the boat and headed back. Thank goodness we speak German, or I have no idea how we would have managed to get out of that situation.

May 25, 1997

For the first time, I find myself at a loss for the right words to describe what has happened in the past three hours or so. When we got off the train in Budapest, we waited for the metro to take us to the train station.

The metro took forever to arrive. When it did, there were tons of people. We squeezed in with the crowd and got smashed inside, with people everywhere.

I wish we would never have gotten on with so many people. It's something we will never do again.

There were two men standing very close to us on the metro. One of the men had extremely bad breath and kept looking down at my fanny pack and my camera hanging from my neck. I kept my hands over them, so he couldn't get to them without being obvious.

Unfortunately, Clarissa wasn't so lucky. One guy pinned her against the wall, while the other guy was feeling for her stuff. They must have been working as a team and were good at it, too.

If only their plan had failed, but unfortunately, it didn't. When we got off the metro, she was telling me how the guy was feeling around for her stuff. Then she looked down and saw that her wallet was gone from her satchel.

I wish we could do things over again and not get onto that crowded metro. It is the easiest thing to get robbed that way. We should have avoided the crowds, plastered ourselves next to one another, and not used a satchel that was so easy to unzip. But we didn't. Clarissa could have held onto her stuff better, too, but she just didn't know.

Thieves like these men don't want anything messy. They don't want you screaming and noticing. They just want to slide the money away without you noticing, which was exactly what happened. The guy even zipped the satchel back up again before making his getaway!

I have to admit, we let down our guard in the metro station. At the beginning of our trip to Budapest, we watched our stuff like crazy everywhere we went – especially when there were people in close proximity. The truth was, by the time we got on that last metro, we had started to trust people – and get too comfortable.

In fact, as we were waiting for the metro, we were on a high, talking about everything we had done and plotting more travels. In our blissful exhilaration, we made ourselves a target.

Like the Matterhorn after the avalanche, Budapest looks different to us now. We were so fascinated, and now it just seems scary.

The more I think about it, the madder I become. And the more afraid I get, the less I believe in the people in this world.

I don't think Clarissa and I will ever feel the same about this place as we did before. For 6,000 forints, those men impacted our trip and our attitudes in a major way. They caused a major hassle for us, too. In addition to the cash, she lost her apartment key (1,500 deutsche marks to replace), credit cards and phone card (useless because we were able to get them stopped), and driver's license.

The whole situation keeps haunting me, and I can't help feeling paranoid about everyone I see. I know the whole thing was so preventable, but it still makes me sick – and very scared. The vulnerable feeling I had when we were stuck in Plochingen has returned. The only difference is that only money was in question this time. That was all they wanted.

I keep thinking about the smooth and heartless way he slipped her wallet – and sense of well-being – right out of her pocket. Some people will do anything for money. I don't want to be there to see someone who wants it more desperately than they did. I can't imagine what they might be capable of.

When we discovered what had happened, Clarissa started crying and had no idea where to turn. The guy in the money exchange booth spoke a little English and showed us to the police station. I filled out a form about the whole thing. Then, we had to figure out how to stop the credit card because they wouldn't let us make calls from their phone, and we didn't even know the credit card number.

An American woman with a huge lock on her fanny pack saw us and asked if she could help. She said she'd also been pickpocketed and didn't trust anyone. I felt bad about her saying that in front of the Hungarian guy who had been so helpful, but I guess he must understand the situation. She called the phone company for us, and Clarissa made a collect call to her neighbor because her parents were unreachable on vacation.

While the neighbor was dealing with the credit card problem, it hit me that the check slip for our luggage had also been in Clarissa's wallet. We both feared our luggage would be gone, although I prayed the guy wouldn't bother since money was probably what he really wanted.

There was nothing to do but go to the police station to file a statement to get the luggage back. By then, we were cutting it close for our train. It was scheduled to leave in half an hour. The police were so painfully slow. One of the officers interpreted, part in English, part in German, as they put an official police report in the computer.

We watched the sheath of computer paper feed slowly through the printer. The printer went through page after page in the spiral. Ever-so-slowly it printed, almost too faintly to be legible.

Clarissa had to sign her name multiple times on different forms. When she was finally done, we watched helplessly as they painstakingly ripped off every last perforated edge of the paper, one at a time.

Finally, we were able to take the police report to the luggage room after frantically running around trying to find it. They wanted to see our passports, which took forever. We pleaded with the manager, and finally, he felt sorry for us, gave us our luggage, and let us go.

The train was about to pull away at any moment. We ran with all our might toward that train, our big backpacks bumping up and down on our backs. More than anything in this world, we did not want to miss that train.

I reached the very last car of the train, just ahead of Clarissa, and grabbed for the handle. Clarissa was following behind me, still not thinking straight. "Is this the right car?" she called.

"Get on the train!" I barked and pulled myself up into the open door. She was right behind me, grasping the handle, pulling herself up into the small space. Just at that moment, the train pulled away from the platform. We jostled through compartment after compartment, not caring how far away we were this time. We were on the train!

After a while, Clarissa fell asleep, but I lay awake, snatches of all that had happened cycling through my mind. A Hungarian student was sharing our compartment, and we started talking. He told me that he studied music in Germany. Then, he started to talk about what tough times the people were going through.

I started to see how the money gained through tourism doesn't come back to most people, but the higher prices affect everyone. I wondered how he could afford to travel. He said that in Germany, he gets a stipend and shares an apartment with two other Hungarians, so he gets by.

Having noticed him traveling with a big cooler of food, I turned the conversation to a lighter subject about how delicious Hungarian food is. He said that he misses the food so much that he always brings as much as he can back with him to Germany. I agreed with him that the food was unlike anything I'd ever experienced before. It still floored me how even the subway station could be filled with such delicious aromas.

Haunted by the memories of those horrible men in the subway, I spent a fateful night filled with visions of him pressing against me and breathing on me with his disgusting breath. We had been so excited before we got on that metro. I just can't believe how much they took from us.

I'm just glad those men didn't take our bags, because my other diary was in there. More than anything else in that bag, I wouldn't want to lose that. As long as I live, I never want to lose a single one of my diaries. I still dream of writing a book someday.

That subway ride, which cost Clarissa money, credit cards, and other immaterial things, keeps playing in my mind. My head is spinning about what I could have done to prevent what happened. Some lessons are learned the hard way, I guess.

This entire trip has been a learning experience, though I could have lived without the last part. I found a couple of dollars worth of spare change in my pockets, and I wish now that I could have given it to someone. It's worthless to me at this point and could have made a difference for someone, but there wasn't time.

I need some time to clear my head. We've done so much; it's hard to fathom. After all we've been through, it's a relief to be back in Germany now, where I feel normal and not so distinctly different as I did in Hungary. Clarissa put it best when she said that she never thought a foreign country could feel so much like home.

Secrets from My Travel Diaries

> ➢ *The way you experience a place changes with the times.*

> ➢ *Some lessons are painful but teach us what we most need to learn.*

> ➢ *You cannot control the unforeseen, but you can choose to set yourself free from it.*

CHAPTER 17

At the Top of the World (Sweden and Denmark)

"I came here with few expectations, as I've learned that
expectations of any kind ruin many experiences."

May 28, 1997

It feels like we have become nomads these past months. After a stopover of only a couple of days, we are already off again and are on yet another train.

I realize now that squeezing in this trip has been too much. There was nothing I wanted to give up, though, and it's too late to turn back now. Anyway, we had to make good on our promise to our college friends, Maja and Sonia, that we'd visit them in Sweden and Denmark.

Maja is Swedish and spent last year at our university in Ohio on an exchange program. Sonia is from the U.S., graduated last year, and returned to Denmark to be with her Danish boyfriend, whom she met while studying abroad in her junior year. (I can't even imagine doing that!)

We spent the night on the train to Denmark, packed like sardines into a small compartment. It was Clarissa, me, a German woman, and an annoying couple wedged in between us. The couple was huddled together, constantly touching each other and kissing. (We were tired enough to get some real sleep, though.)

When we got on the train from Hamburg to Copenhagen, Denmark, Clarissa and I were amazed when the train drove right onto the ferry, to get across the water. We seemed to be the only ones amazed by this, though. Everyone else just sat calmly while we crammed ourselves into the space between the train and the side of the ferry and took pictures.

A Swedish student came up to us while we were taking pictures. It turned out she goes to the university in Lund, just like Maja does. She got us even more excited by telling us all about Sweden and what it was like to go to the university.

When we arrived in Copenhagen, Sonia met us at the station to see us off onto the ferry to Malmo. We walked with her through a dreary rain, but I barely noticed it. It was so much fun listening to her tell us all about Copenhagen. She seemed so worldly from the whole experience of studying abroad and living in Denmark. I guess we are becoming that way, too.

The ferry ride between Denmark and Sweden was only about 15 minutes long. When we arrived in Sweden, Maja met us at the ferry dock and took us to her dorm. She has a big dorm room with her own bathroom and a shower down the hall.

Through a small corridor, she shares a kitchen with eight other students. It was a really nice place, and way nicer than most of the hostels we've stayed in.

Maja served us bread with this wonderful Gouda cheese with tomatoes on top and the best tea I've ever tasted. It was positively wonderful, after traveling for so long and getting caught in the rain. I never knew I liked tea, but it was so good in Scandinavia, especially with the dreary weather.

She was going to a soccer game with a couple of friends and invited us to go, but we were exhausted. When she returned a couple of hours after our nap, we went to dinner at her "Nation."

"Nations" are like sororities, except that they are both guys and girls together and are very large. Hers had about 1,500 people. Everyone at the university is involved in one, and each has its own activities, like student-made dinners, parties, and excursions.

It seemed like a great way to get everyone involved and to be able to do things at a cheaper price, as Scandinavian prices seemed pretty out of control. Dinner at the Nation was excellent, but even there, our meal wasn't cheap, at about $10.

After breakfast, we walked around Lund for most of the afternoon, looking at the shops, gardens, and a cathedral. The weather was beautiful, a gorgeous day to be in that wonderful, cobblestoned, Scandinavian world. It was another place with a different vibe entirely from the ones we'd been in before.

When we got back to Maja's apartment, we got ready and went to a party with her Nation. I always felt like I wasn't dressed classy enough for Vienna when we were there. But at the party in Sweden, everything seemed to work when it came to dress. Some people were in cocktail dresses or ties, others in jeans and tennis shoes. Everybody was friendly and good at speaking English. Maja said that a lot of their textbooks, and even some of the presentations they have to give in school, are in English, so they get used to it.

Dinner was exotic and didn't seem "student-made" at all. The first course was tomato soup, which had chunks of onions, tomatoes, and spices and tasted totally different from American tomato soup. Then we had Ostrich, which I guess is all the rage in Scandinavia. It tasted like a chewier steak. On top was a sweet sauce, which I think is called *remoulade*, with a potato wrap on the side. For dessert, we had pineapple parfait and coffee.

Along with the meal, we drank beer and had these strong, fruity shots they called "punch." Then the Swedish drinking songs began. We danced for hours. They also played some songs from England, which I guess have been very popular in Sweden for the past couple of years, but had never made it to America.

One of the songs they played is apparently number one in the U.S., but it was the first time I'd heard it. It's funny how they release different songs in different countries. I guess we've missed a lot of the "latest" in the U.S. since we've been away.

Afterward, we watched David Letterman in English with Swedish subtitles, talked for a while, and went to bed. It was fun seeing an episode that was only a week old. I'm not even sure what we have available in Germany. Although I have a TV in my apartment, I've never sat down to watch it. I never seem to have time.

The next day, we picked up Sonia at the ferry dock and stopped by Maja's parent's house to pick up their car for the day. Sonia was able to carry on a conversation with Maja's mom because she could speak to her in Danish and understand Maja's mom's reply in Swedish. It's amazing how similar the Scandinavian languages and Dutch are to one another. Here and there, I could even pick out a few words that sounded like German.

We went to a place called Vik on the east coast of Sweden and had a wonderful picnic that Maja's mom had prepared. It was the most incredible, freeing feeling to be driven around without a care in the world about where we were going, and to have such wonderful food provided for us. There is something to be said for coming into a trip with no expectations and just being along for the ride.

The ocean was beautiful, a deep blue like I'd never seen before. We walked down the rocky shoreline to see a mysterious crater, which Maja said no one knew why it was there or how it had formed. The shoreline was edged with fossils unique to the area.

After that, we got back in the car and wound around and up and down the country roads of Sweden, pulling over to check out whatever we pleased. We stopped at a beautiful sandy beach, where people were swimming all around, but it was way too cold for us. Then, we continued through the countryside, which was lined with apple trees, rolling green hills, and fields upon fields of yellow flowers as far as we could see.

I guess the yellow flowers are grown for vegetable oil. No matter what the purpose, they were gorgeous. We got out, and Clarissa and I got our pictures taken in a field of them, getting pollen all over our clothes. (I think the photo will be good, though.)

When we got back in the car, "Top of the World" came on the radio. It was the perfect song to capture the moment. All four of us sang in one full voice as we wound up and down the road through the hills of bright yellow flowers.

My heart felt so full, between the beauty all around and the bond between us. I thought, "This is what it feels like to be free. This was what it meant to be at the top of the world!" I wanted the moment to last forever.

When we got back to Malmo, we went to a barbecue with a bunch of students from Maja's Nation. It was set atop a hill with an amazing view looking out over Lund, Malmo, and Copenhagen.

The sun set over our hill at around a quarter to ten. We were so far north that the sky didn't even need the sun to be light. Even in the middle of the night, it was a deep blue color and not totally dark.

On the way back, we stopped for tea at Maja's friend's apartment. She created this incredibly magical ambiance by lighting candles everywhere. We talked about how Scandinavian culture is very *into* creating atmosphere, and how the dim lighting creates a feeling of coziness throughout the long, dark winters.

June 1, 1997

Clarissa and I took the ferry back to Copenhagen with Sonia. She bid us farewell by treating us to Danish ice cream with whipped cream on top and a dollop of jam instead of a cherry.

Clarissa and I spent the rest of the day exploring Copenhagen before catching the night train back to Freiburg. We took a canal boat tour to get an overview of the city since it was such a beautiful day. Then, we walked around, just experiencing Copenhagen. The city was so full of people and excitement.

Down by the harbor, there were rows of restaurants, so we split a "typical" meal of redskin sausage at a rather expensive place. It was a perfect day just to sit, eat, lounge around, and spend every last cent of Danish money we had.

At a nearby table, we noticed two people pouring over their *Let's Go* book, oblivious to the surroundings. It made me think of how much we've changed the way we travel since those first trips we took. We've learned that it's far more interesting to *experience* places instead of simply seeing them. And with your nose stuck in a guidebook, you miss what the day has to offer.

In some ways, Sweden and Denmark have felt more like the U.S. than the other countries we've visited. Maja is Swedish, but because we knew her from our university, being with her felt like being back in the U.S. – I'm not sure how much of that feeling was simply because we were with Maja and Sonia the whole time.

Sonia seems like a cross between American and European to me now. She has so many insights into things I'd never thought about. We talked about how much Sweden – especially the university students – seemed like they were living in a utopia. Everyone seemed so happy everywhere we went. She remarked that even the way people talked was so happy and polite sounding.

Everyone we met was so friendly and interested in us. I felt really at home there – on top of the world – even with my own home so far away.

Secrets from My Travel Diaries

> ➢ *Don't forgo the opportunity to pay a visit to your friends in another country.*

> ➢ *Hills of yellow flowers may look beautiful from afar, but they'll cover you with sticky pollen when you get in their midst.*

> ➢ *You can feel at home wherever you are when you're with people who fill you up.*

CHAPTER 18

Not Everything Has Changed
(Lutherstadt Wittenberg, Germany)

"I really love it here … I'd forgotten how much."

June 5, 1997

Clarissa and I are sitting on the same bench in the train station in Halle that we sat in two years ago, when we studied in *Lutherstadt* Wittenberg [Luther City Wittenberg] in the summer of 1995. We're going to visit our host families for *Stadtfest* [City Festival] weekend. Within the next hour, we should be there, after changing trains one more time.

Lutherstadt Wittenberg, the sister city of Wittenberg University, my university in Ohio, was part of East Germany and inaccessible for decades. The summer program that Clarissa and I attended was one of the first after the program reopened.

We lived with host families and attended classes every day, taught in German by German professors. The curriculum was customized for us and included local economics, history, and language. It was a true immersion, as most people spoke Russian as their second language instead of English.

Lutherstadt Wittenberg seemed to me like a place still caught between two worlds. It felt like the older generation was in a time warp, and many people struggled with all the change. Meanwhile, the younger generation came from a different place and time entirely, with different views of the world and their place in it.

Nevertheless, the townspeople welcomed me with open arms that summer. I got to know people from all over town, and we shared a sort of mutual fascination with one another. They made me feel at home, even though the place I called home was somewhere they could not even imagine.

Waking up this morning on the train, I could see the familiar flatness of the land and the gray, austere buildings – remnants of Communism that I'd become so used to two summers ago. Wittenberg is such a different world than Freiburg, but in a lot of ways, being here feels like coming home again.

So much is changing for me now; it feels like nothing is staying the same. Our semester in Freiburg is already ending soon, then I'll be going to Paris, graduating, and starting my career.

I wonder what has happened in Wittenberg over the past two years. It would be so nice to be going back to a place where at least most things have stayed the same. Not sure what else has changed, but I hope, at least, that everyone I knew and loved is still there.

June 6, 1997

We have been greeted with such a warm welcome here. All we've done is eat (pretty much perpetually!) and catch up with seemingly everyone in town. Everyone has been fussing over us, which is even more special because it's been so long since we've been in a family setting.

When we arrived in Wittenberg, Clarissa's host dad picked us up. We had a wonderful breakfast at their house, then slept for a few hours. Clarissa's host mom had *Döner Kebabs* waiting for us when we woke up, and they tasted so good. Then she got out two extra bikes, and the three of us rode to the city center. That felt so incredibly good! I hadn't realized how much I'd missed the small-town feel of riding bikes everywhere.

In the city center, there were all types of makeshift stands, with people selling things. Clarissa still had no wallet, and I hadn't been able to replace the scrunchie that blew away in Budapest. We were able to buy both for really good prices. (I wish Freiburg had the prices that they have here. Everything in Wittenberg seems to cost about half as much as it does in Freiburg.)

The guy selling the scrunchies asked me where I was from. When I told him, he got really excited and started asking me all about the U.S. Then, he insisted I pick out any scrunchie I wanted for free. I guess it is still a big thing to see Americans traveling here!

When we returned, Clarissa's host mom had dinner ready. I didn't want to eat much because my host family [the Müllers: Günther, Lina, Tobias, and Katrin] were picking me up to stay for the weekend, and they were having a barbeque.

Clarissa's host mom insisted I have a bite, anyway. She had made me a cappuccino, too, knowing how much I love them. I felt self-conscious eating at the table, with Günther watching me from across the room in a chair against the wall, when he came shortly after to pick me up.

I drank the cappuccino as fast as I could, but it was difficult because it was so hot, and so hot outside, too. (Having the iced version would seem refreshing on a hot summer day, but that just doesn't seem to be what they do here.)

June 8, 1997

This has been the most wonderful weekend I have ever imagined. I never knew how much homesickness I would have for Wittenberg. It's too bad that Freiburg is so far away. Nine hours by train is too long and expensive to come frequently.

It's so comforting to go where everything is exactly how I so fondly remember it. Not much seems to have changed over these past two years, except that the kids are older now. All the same people, food, and parties were still here for me. I appreciate everyone here so much now. They are truly the most hospitable and generous people I could ever imagine.

I feel like I ate my way through the weekend. On Saturday morning, I slept late. This created the same problem I had two summers ago: being served breakfast when I got up and then lunch an hour later.

About ten of the Müllers' relatives poured in for lunch, then we all headed to *Stadtfest*. There was a big parade and all kinds of tents, with a Middle Ages theme reminiscent of Martin Luther. Walking around all afternoon in the hot sun was incredibly hot, but it was so much fun to be with them again that nothing else mattered.

The afternoon *Stadtfest* was followed by another barbeque that lasted through the evening. I stuffed myself with the *Wurst* (sausage), shish kebabs, and salad that I'd loved so much.

Nadine and Dennis, who I'd met through my other host family, the Webers, biked over and invited me to a pig roast. I borrowed Lina's bike and went with them.

It was another big reunion, with about 20 of them who hang out regularly. They are all so close, even though it's a big group. It must be so much more fun to have such a close-knit friend group and always have something to do in such a sleepy town.

Like my host family, they remembered all my likes and dislikes and had my favorites waiting for me. Nadine and Dennis even brought me a bottle of *Honigwein* [honey wine] to take home to my parents.

We sat by the fire, with the huge pig cooking over it, and reminisced about all the good times we'd had. Then, we caught up on everything that had happened over the past two years. The change I saw in them was that they had a broader perspective. As it did for me, it came from traveling and hearing about different places they didn't know before.

One of the other guys, Jörg, camped out next to me for a while, cracking jokes and talking about the things he knew about America. Every time he thought of a word in English that he knew, he'd randomly yell it out in the middle of the conversation. "Yellowstone!" he cried out once, in a loud voice, and we all laughed.

What made it funnier was that oftentimes he would pronounce the word in a way that I didn't understand at first. I'd think about it for a moment, and then I'd realize what he meant and say, "Ohhhh. . ." and repeat the name again with my accent. Then he'd make fun of how I said it.

This continued again and again. He kept telling me that the whole group was going to come to America to visit me and speak nothing but English. Everyone laughed over the whole thing, and we had a great time.

Later, I got out my Tom Petty tape, and we started playing *Wildflowers*. It was the first time I'd listened to it in a while. People kept hitting the stop button on the tape, asking me to translate the song line by line. It was so fun to think that they could share my love for that song because of my translations.

I can't even describe how marvelous it was to be with the whole crowd again; I felt so at home. It made me wonder why I feel the need to go to Paris on this quest to "find myself." I should just come back here for the rest of the summer.

Günther says that it is always so enjoyable to have me and that I can always come back when I want to. I know he means that. I truly love their family and everyone else I've met here. I really wish I didn't have to leave after this weekend.

Nadine and Dennis biked back to my host family's house with me around three-thirty in the morning. I had to sleep in the kids' room because all ten relatives stayed overnight after *Stadtfest*. Even with so many people around, it never felt really cramped, and I always felt completely welcome and included.

I had fun playing with the kids, too. They loved having me sleeping in their room and used me as a prop for whatever they could imagine. Katrin wanted to play that I was sick and that she was the nurse. Lina burst out laughing when she came in to find Katrin bending over me, taking my temperature as I lay "sick" in her bed.

After breakfast with the huge group of extended family, it was time to transition to staying with my other host family, the Webers. Renata arrived half an hour early to pick me up and had to sit and wait for me while I finished breakfast (again!).

I said a regretful goodbye to everyone. Then Renata and I left, arriving at her house just in time for lunch, which I didn't eat much of, for obvious reasons. Since I'd last been there, her house had been totally reconstructed to the point where everyone had to move out for six months to get it done. Everything was new and looked so beautiful.

Renata's husband Wolfgang was only around for about an hour before he had to leave to catch the train back to Frankfurt. The economy is still pretty tough here, so when he lost his job, he could find nothing in the area. Now, he works in Frankfurt, stays with his son and family, and only gets to come home every two weeks.

I was always more comfortable with Renata, anyway, though. She always seemed to me like a friend, more than a host mom.

That afternoon after coffee and cake, Renata and her mom, and I went back for the end of *Stadtfest*. We walked around for a bit, had a huge sundae at an outdoor café, and then came back to the house and had dinner.

After dinner, we talked for a long time, taking shots from a bottle that Renata had brought back from her vacation in Puerto Rico. Her mother downed the shots, even though the alcohol was strong.

Eventually, her mom went to bed, and Renata and I continued talking for hours. I instantly remembered how easy it always was to talk to Renata and how much we laugh together. Our relationship is full of openness and easy, flowing conversation, like I feel with Clarissa and Anne.

The Müllers mean a lot to me, too, but being with them is so drastically different. Yesterday, for example, the entire family and I ate shish kebabs at the barbeque in total silence. Granted, shish kebabs can be messy, and they take concentration to eat, but the silence is an adjustment for me.

I've learned from the Müllers to stop trying overly hard to fill the silence or worry about how the conversation is (or isn't) going. I've realized that theirs is a comfortable silence. It's just how they are and what they do.

The weekend is over now, and I am sitting here on the train, feeling downright nostalgic about leaving. Renata had a tear in her eye when I left. We were both so sad! I know it's doubly hard for her now that her kids are grown up, and even her husband is away most of the time. I've resolved to find at least one extra week to return to Wittenberg before leaving for the U.S.

As a memento of this weekend, sitting between Clarissa and me is a bag filled with food that Renata sent back with me. I think we ate more this weekend than I normally would in about a week.

After this constant eating, my jeans feel a little tight. (I don't think I can blame it on them shrinking from all the cycles in those crummy Freiburg washers…) It was all so worth it, though.

As I sit here on this train with a full stomach and a full heart, I'm overcome by the feeling that life really is about what and who makes you feel free. It's about the people who keep you moving forward, instead of chained to the drudgery of life. They are the ones who get you to really *live* – instead of looking back later with nothing to say but, "If only…" in a wistful way.

I'm finding it so difficult to accept that, within the next month, things will be so different. By mid-July, almost no one I know will be left in Freiburg.

Almost no one I know will be there next year. The international students will all be gone. In addition, one of my German suitemates got a yearlong stipend to go to America for the next school year. A couple of others will be transferring to a different school.

How incredible it was to step back into the life and relationships I knew two years ago, with everyone still right where they were when I left! What a comfort to know that, at least in Wittenberg, things had stayed relatively the same.

This weekend, I got so many invitations to be a part of so many fun things. I'll have to miss all of them. As Günther said the other night, though: "Every time you're in one place, you invariably miss something somewhere else, and you just can't do it all."

I really wish I could, though!

It's so hard to accept that everything will change so drastically soon. It's amazing how life twists and turns so much. At least, for this one wonderful weekend, it felt as though some things had stayed the same...

Secrets from My Travel Diaries

> ➢ *Life is about what – and who – makes you feel free.*

> ➢ *The people in your life help you make sense of an ever-changing world.*

> ➢ *You just can't do it all.*

CHAPTER 19

You Get What You Negotiate

"All I really want to do is sit outside and read one romance novel after another. For better or worse, I'll have to put that on hold for now. Too much to do… so little desire to do it!"

June 10, 1997

Back in Freiburg, I feel so disconnected from my life here. After traveling in every direction since the 1st of May, it seems like eons ago since we were here for more than a few days in a row. My last real memory of what (used to be) normal life here is when Clarissa, Anne, and I cooked gnocchi right before Switzerland.

I know somehow I'll settle back in and re-establish my relationships with my flatmates – and do what I need to do to wrap up the semester with good grades, too. At least my test in *Hören und Sprechen* didn't go too badly. I was pretty nervous about that because I'm often a little lost in that class.

June 13, 1997

So many thoughts have been running through my head. Earlier today, I spent almost two hours emailing people back home. Right now, I'm sitting by a tree, not feeling like doing anything. I'm just here, soaking up the sun.

I've yet to feel such a tug from home as I do right now. As I sit here, I feel so down because I'm missing my brother's graduation party. I would love to be there. If only I could parachute in and enjoy the comforts of home again for a couple of days and then come right back.

At least one good thing about going back home will be that I'll appreciate it more. I'm looking forward to everyone and everything waiting for me there. Over the course of these months, I've really realized the people who are most important to me.

June 16, 1997

It's nice not to have to deal with each class more than one day a week or so. Having Fridays open has really made my experience here, too. Still, the long days – especially Mondays – are hard to sit through.

The German university system operates so differently from what I'm used to. It seems like the German students I've met have been going to university for years and are in no hurry to get out. In the U.S., it's way too expensive to do that.

The grading system is so different, too. In Germany, they serve up these massive exams that cover large amounts of material well outside the timeframe of a U.S. semester. For the classes I'm taking directly at the university, the professors don't seem to understand our grading scale and have no idea how to even arrive at a grade within just a few months.

I'm realizing I will have to advocate for myself for each *Schein* [grade certificate] I get for my transcript. I hate negotiating with each professor for my grade, but there's nothing else I can do. As long as it all works out in the end, I guess it's okay.

It's very frustrating to do so much work and feel so much stress, instead of enjoying my last days here. When I think of all the work ahead, I feel like I want to fly off somewhere warm, like Greece or southern Spain, sit on a beach, and just disappear from the rest of the world for a while. I can never seem to escape from the pressures of grades – or from the pressure I put on myself.

I have so much to do and so little desire to do it. It's so difficult to get work done here. I guess I'm just burned out, and it doesn't help that some of the professors don't seem to care, either. I need to let go of all this pressure, do what I need to do, and enjoy my remaining time. It's just getting more and more difficult to let myself go, because everything I have to do keeps looming.

Adding to that is how incredibly muggy it is outside. There isn't much relief inside, either, with no air conditioning. I wonder if I can make it these last few weeks without breaking down and buying a fan. Every summer I'm in Europe, I'm quickly reminded of how difficult it is to keep cool here. It's so hot. I feel like I have no energy to accomplish anything.

Hören und Sprechen is one of the few classes we've had regular tests. On the most recent test, I got a "3" on my French pronunciation and failed the transcription because the professor counted off every little error. I feel so helpless because I can't understand the tapes well, and spending more time studying doesn't even seem to help.

I went to see the professor, *Herr* [Mr.] Fuchs, during his office hours, and we discussed my grade. He threatened to fail me if I didn't work harder and turn in some extra assignments. That flipped me out. I can't imagine getting a failing grade on my transcript.

After our conversation, I quickly declared the class pass/fail, so at least I wouldn't have to worry about the grade. Then, I talked to Amelie, the French student who had helped me with my resume, to see if she could assist. My only hope is to boost my pronunciation grade and hand in the extra assignments and transcriptions. I just hope the transcription on the next test isn't completely impossible this time.

A similar grading challenge happened in Theater class. The professor made a special announcement for the "*Amerikaner* [Americans]." She said she was sorry that she hadn't known about the difference in the grading system and that if we did an extra paper, she would adjust our grades.

I worked for two and a half days on the extra Theater paper, but once I had the draft, I reread it and decided that I hated it. I'd had so much trouble focusing that it wasn't organized and concise.

After that, the "studious me" returned out of necessity, so I didn't fail all my classes. I went to the program office to use the computer and went crazy with the cut-and-paste buttons, reorganizing everything until I liked it again. Then, Hilda corrected it for me. She really liked it and said it sounded so "sophisticated." I felt so stressed about it yesterday; it was a relief when she said that today.

I asked my *Wirtschaft* [Business] professor if I could do an extra paper to pull up my grade in that class, too. She assigned me to write about the American school system. That paper is due in a week, which is definitely a lot of pressure but attainable. I camped out for nearly eight hours at the program office writing it, then spent time this weekend editing it from the printed version.

I've been a little disheartened ever since I asked her about the B I got on my midterm. She admitted she'd looked at who had the most pages and assigned the grades accordingly. I guess I'll have to write bigger next time. (Luckily, this paper is typed instead of handwritten, so that I won't have that problem.)

When I leave Freiburg, I know I'll miss it. But right now, I'd like nothing more than to dump all these awful classes and just read romance novels. It seems crazy that every day is not only bringing me closer to freedom from these dreaded classes, but also closer to closing this chapter of my life.

June 23, 1997

Two classes, Theater and Market Integration, are completely done now, which feels so good. Both of them went fine, I think. I was strategic about being the last one to finish the Market Integration final so that I could talk to the professor about the U.S. grading scale. He glanced through my final, said that it looked good, and then said, *"Alles Klar"* ["Understood"]. I think that's a good sign.

As I was dropping something off at the program office, I started talking with the program administrator about my anxieties over failing French, too. She told me I should enjoy my time here and everything would work out fine. (Since she's the one who administers the program and oversees everything that goes on, I felt better about it then.)

I hate having to ask for and negotiate for my grades, but there's nothing else I can do. I do know that I earned the grades I'm getting, though, according to the U.S. system. The professors simply don't know how to grade me until I tell them because the entire approach is so different. It's all ridiculous, and there is probably more negotiating ahead for me, but I'll do what I have to do.

June 24, 1997

I really had to get my butt in gear to get my *Schein* in my Religions of the World class. It's definitely my least favorite class. The class meets twice a week, but fortunately, one of the days it meets is Thursday. This helped preserve my sanity because almost every Thursday in May was a holiday.

The professor, *Herr* Hahn, reads in a monotone the entire time, without even looking up, and it is so difficult to follow. The whole thing is so far beyond the German vocabulary I've needed thus far for day-to-day living.

At the end of every lecture, he proceeds to layer on a vast amount of reading material as homework. I was totally overwhelmed until I learned that some of the material was only "suggested" and that you were expected to go deeper according to your interests.

That made things even more difficult, though, because I didn't know how I could get a grade that way. There have been no exams or graded assignments in that class at all.

To have a way to grade the American students, *Herr* Hahn decided to have each of us schedule 15-minute interviews for him to ask us questions. I hoped he would ask about something I knew well enough to speak intelligently about.

One German student, Emil, was assigned to help the American students weed through the lecture material and prepare. He was a big help and even sat in the interview with me.

My interview with *Herr* Hahn lasted 30 minutes instead of 15, mainly because, similar to his lectures, he kept talking and talking. Occasionally, he would ask some random question that was nothing like what I'd spent so long studying.

I felt like I was going to pass out halfway through, and when it was over, I was convinced I'd failed. My voice was shaking, but I forced myself to sit up straight and at least find some way to answer, even if I didn't completely know what to say. I just kept going the best I could.

Finally, *Herr* Hahn seemed satisfied with my answers and started asking me what made me decide to study in Freiburg. I told him about studying in

Lutherstadt Wittenberg and connected the dots with the Religions of the World class, which wasn't lost on him.

When we wrapped up, I asked him about the grading process, and he told me he was going to give me a B+. That was probably a gift, considering the number of intelligent things I had to say. I'll take it!

Emil and I walked out of that office, feeling victorious to have gotten through the exam. Sometimes I didn't even understand what the professor was talking about, let alone be able to answer his question. Still, I just kept going, found something to say, and didn't let it shake my confidence. Ultimately, everything worked out. That is all that matters.

June 25, 1997

My friends have nothing to do anymore. They're all busy going out and shopping for souvenirs and having a good time. It is really sickening how much work I've had to do because of the pressures of my GPA. I wish I could be doing what they're doing instead.

The only thing that makes studying easier is that it rains every day. The weather has turned cold, too. Now I'm wearing heavier clothes than I did for parts of February.

Today was my day to get my final grade in my dreaded *Hören und Sprechen* class. I spent another two hours with Amelie beforehand, transcribing the news and working on pronunciation. She is so patient and has really been a lifesaver, between helping me avoid failing French and proofreading my resume and cover letter.

During my final day in his class, the professor kept calling on me, the lone *Amerikaner* in the class. It was nerve-racking. However, at the end of class, he announced to everyone that it was my last day in the class, and they all looked sad.

I had to stay after class for about two hours to take the final French test. When I came out after the test, a big group of people from the class were waiting for me, and we all went to the *Mensa* together. We talked for a long while and exchanged addresses.

Despite the torture it often was to have no clue how to transcribe the news in French, I really have met some very cool people in that class. And one way or another, I am now officially free of French class in Germany.

June 27, 1997

Everyone else went out to a party, but I couldn't go because I was studying day and night for my *Wirtschaft* [Business] exam. (Luckily, the party wasn't that much fun, and everyone came back early, so I didn't feel like I missed too much.)

I'd been studying off and on for weeks. There's so much memorizing that I could have recited the stuff in my sleep. I got a 1.5 on my test and a 1.2 as a final grade, with a note from the professor that she really liked my paper. (The German grading scale goes from 1 to 6, with 1 being the highest.)

It was nice to get some recognition for how hard I worked in that class. I really needed that equivalent of an "A" for my GPA.

I am officially done with my exams now. It looks like I passed everything and got good enough grades to maintain my GPA, too. I really did learn a lot in those classes, even if, in some cases, it was largely due to my own effort. It would have been nice not to have to work quite so hard, though.

Tonight, Anne, Clarissa, Mike, Tom, and I celebrated the successful end of the semester by making *"amerikanisches Essen"* [American food] and inviting our *Mitbewohner* [flatmates]. We decided to prepare an American breakfast: eggs with mushrooms and onions, pancakes and maple syrup, home fries, toast, bacon, and orange juice. For dessert, we served doughnuts from a mix we'd gotten from the American section of the grocery store.

It was quite a project, fraught with cross-cultural cooking mishaps. At one point, we had all four stove burners covered with two batches of potatoes, pancakes, and scrambled eggs; bacon in the oven with tin foil since it wouldn't fit on the stove; and toast popping out of the toaster.

We decided to make our own pancake mix because the pre-made stuff was an outrageous 10 deutsche marks [about $6] for a tiny package. Making the pancake batter was a big challenge because we didn't have a recipe and had to guess what to do.

Mike, Tom, and Anne had play practice, and I had to return to the university to get my *Hören und Sprechen Schein*. This meant that, initially, Clarissa was left to take charge of pretty much the whole thing.

I walked into the kitchen just as Clarissa's first pancake attempt was coming off the griddle. The batter was like rubber and had huge clumps of butter in it that hadn't been mixed in. I stepped in to help and kept adding more sugar, flour, an occasional egg, milk, and water to the batter.

With every attempt, the pancakes got less rubbery. Finally, we got one that tasted right. The huge bowl of batter quickly turned into heaps of pancakes, which were almost the right texture, tasted good, and ultimately were eagerly consumed.

Never imagining how long it would really take to make all that stuff, we ended up serving the *"amerikanisches Essen"* at eleven-thirty at night instead of ten o'clock like we'd planned. Everyone was really nice about the wait and said it didn't matter how long it took as long as it tasted good.

Our *Mitbewohner* loved everything except the maple syrup, which they thought was disgusting. Hilda decided to wrap her pancake in a roll and put jelly in the middle, which tasted better to me, too. (I'm very particular about syrup, and I have to say, the one brand we could find wasn't all that good.)

We stayed and talked for another couple of hours, and then I had to run around again in the morning and pick up my *Wirtschaft Schein*, make copies of my French resume, and buy a bunch of German books at *Kaufhof* during their "4 deutsche marks" sale.

So, now, here I am, finished with the semester. I worked really hard and pushed through. I advocated for myself and my grades when I needed to. The work consumed me for a while, but now it's finished. I am free!

Secrets from My Travel Diaries

➢ *Set your sights on your goals and go after them with confidence and courage.*

➢ *Advocate for yourself and what you want.*

➢ *Just keep going, work hard, and push through.*

CHAPTER 20

Tugs in Opposite Directions...
Who Am I Now?

"Sometimes, even now, I still can't believe that I've had the chance to live here. Other times, being surrounded by historic buildings and people speaking German seems totally normal."

June 28, 1997

We've started photographing everything in Freiburg that seems normal now, but that fascinated us when we first got here. We went all around the city center to all the places we've frequented, including to the travel agency, where we took a picture of Hans. At the *Mensa,* we captured a photo of one of the conveyor belts that whisks the food away.

Because we were rarely around on weekends, we've been catching up on all the tourist things in Freiburg, too. The *Münster Markt* [Münster Market] is a lot bigger and more happening on Saturdays. We went there and had *Wurst* [German sausage], bought various baked goods, and sampled everything.

After that, we climbed up the *Freiburger Münster* [Freiburg Cathedral]. I was struck by how picturesque Freiburg really is. It is easy to get so used to your surroundings that you forget how beautiful they are, until you see them from afar.

Tonight, we tried out the *Spätzle* [German egg noodle] maker that Clarissa had bought to take back to the U.S. (*Spätzle* is amazing because all you need to make it is some flour, water, milk, and eggs. You mix it all together and put it into a special tool that you crank by hand to make the noodles. Then, when you put it in a pot of boiling water, it just floats to the top, and it's done.) We had the best time!

I'm appreciating everyone more and more these days. Traveling with Clarissa and Anne feels like sprinkling fairy dust in the air. That magic wouldn't have been there, had they not been walking next to me.

All along the way, it's been me and my friends and our backpacks and Eurail passes, going all over Europe, seeing and doing whatever catches our fancy. We'd just get on the train, read, sleep, write in our diaries, or laugh about the latest adventure – and then, before we knew it, we'd be at our destination.

Every place we traveled was filled with funny, random things that happened and so many precious moments. We really watched out for each other all along the way.

I can't believe that just days from now, I won't see most of the people that I've gotten to know here – some not for years, others never again. Most live in different parts of the United States and even the world. I guess, no matter what, I'll always know that somewhere out there, wherever we may end up, there are others who share the same stories, the same laughter, and the same experiences that I do.

June 29, 1997

I've been in such a reflective mood. I feel like I'm struggling to stay afloat, with constant tugs in opposite directions.

One tug I'm feeling is back toward my roots: to what's familiar, to everything that I thought I knew, to the way I grew up.

The other tug pulls me toward wandering and seeing and experiencing. That tug pushes me further out into the unknown, to the things that I don't yet understand, to places I don't yet know, to experiences that I haven't yet had.

I was looking through my photo album, and I couldn't help asking myself who was this young woman in the pictures. But there I was, standing next to my friends with a big smile, with all those different places in the backdrop behind me.

It's hard to believe I'm living in a foreign country, in a life that feels very normal now. When I bought my Eurail pass, I couldn't possibly grasp how those trains would take me to the places that I'd only dreamed of. And I didn't know how much going to all those places would change me.

Sometimes everything I've experienced still seems like a dream. Yet that is me in the pictures, standing in front of a windmill in Amsterdam or the Colosseum in Rome. Only my diaries make it feel a little more real.

… but who is this *me*?

Arriving in Freiburg feels like an eternity ago. There have been so many different chapters in these past months. I feel like I was a completely different person experiencing each one of them. I may not look much different on the outside, but inwardly I feel completely different.

These months have brought a series of tiny moments that have altered my way of seeing things forever. It seems like everything I thought I knew was just a fabrication in my own mind. I didn't realize how much I didn't know – and still don't know – about life, economies, and customs worldwide.

As the world has gotten smaller in my view, the people who live in that world seem to have become much more complex. I know a little better what makes people tick and why, but I see now that there's a vast ocean of things I still don't understand.

I feel like I understand myself even less than I did when I arrived. Then again, I didn't know who I was then, either. I just didn't know what I didn't know.

Who was that young woman who got on the plane to Germany on February 19th, 1997? And who is she who will soon board the train on a one-way ticket to Paris? I wonder, too, who will get on the plane and fly back to the United States?

I have no answer.

Today someone yelled across the street to me, "You're beautiful!"

Am I beautiful? I was once convinced I was, based on what I'd been told, but I don't know anymore. There's so much I've been doubting about myself. I no longer know who I see when I look in the mirror.

Who am I? I just don't know. I guess I'm the same person I always was, just with a broader perspective.

There is so much that is stirred up and confused inside. I have a feeling there must be something I was put on this earth to do, and I wonder now if I really do want to go into business or something else entirely.

It remains to be seen if my international business career will feed my curiosity and be what I want. Maybe there are some things that only life and time know the answers to.

What exactly will make me happy? What kind of life... career... man... will light a fire inside me that will keep me going each day for the rest of my life? What kind of career can show me the world but still allow me to develop roots that will be lasting?

Now more than ever, I have no idea.

I do know that I want to live! Not just be alive. I don't want to become so over-ambitious that I forget that. It would be so easy to fall into that trap – I know I have the natural tendency to push myself to the limit.

Even now, my thoughts are already turning to moving on. As the flurry of traveling and studying recedes at last, I find myself standing on the precipice of something else new.

Soon I will face another major change when I go to Paris. Part of me is excited about all the changes ahead. Another part of me just wants everything to stay the same for a while.

I can't fathom what it will be like to put everything I possess into my suitcase and leave an empty room behind. Locking the door behind me for the last time will mean closing this chapter of my life.

I vacillate between wanting to go home now, and desperately wanting to stay. It feels like I'm caught between two worlds. I feel like I don't belong anywhere anymore.

It's as if I keep drifting in and out between the same me I was before and the vastly different me I'm becoming. In traveling the world and learning so much about other cultures, I never imagined that I'd learn so much about myself. I see now that I grew the most when things went wrong, too, as much – as I didn't like it at the time.

Realizations about how much I really have grown are flooding over me in waves. After all that I've been through, when I go back home to what used to be familiar, I don't want to change back into whoever it was that I used to be.

It's so hard to process what I've been through and understand what it all means. But what I do know is that there is beauty all around me, countless blessings that I can only find within myself. I want to keep shining the light within me for the rest of my life.

July 1, 1997

I'm sitting in the middle of a field next to a vineyard that overlooks the mountains. The sun is shining, and Clarissa, Anne, and I are resting in the grass, savoring the moment and happy to be alive.

Today, we finally got back to where Clarissa, Mike, and I got lost the night we went out with Hilda and Mark for the first time. It was absolutely beautiful, with huge, prestigious-looking houses that seemed to be carved out of the mountains. After that, we kept walking back to our favorite spot among the vineyards.

The mountains are not visible from the city center, and I sometimes forget I'm in the middle of them. But here in these vineyards looking out, it is impossible to forget.

Here, reality just melts away. It's as if my surroundings were created only for this brief moment as I gaze upon them and feel whole again.

As I sit here surrounded by the breathtaking beauty and bathed in sunlight, it is so easy to be sure that somehow, some way, everything is exactly as it was meant to be.

July 2, 1997

Tonight, Clarissa and I went out with Fritz, his girlfriend, and a couple of his other friends. Fritz reminded me of how we met in that pub when we first arrived in Germany, and I just had to laugh. I feel like I was another person then. It is such a strange feeling and reminded me again how much I've changed.

I've been so busy I don't think I've even stopped to look at myself in the mirror until recently. Now when I do, I feel like a foreigner in the shadow of my old self. I have left my life in America behind and can see it in a different light. But I still need some more time to think and absorb all that I feel is changing inside.

It was a lot of fun seeing Fritz again. He is one of those genuinely nice people, as is his girlfriend. He kept asking about all the places we'd traveled. It still hasn't even become real yet, that we really were in all those places.

July 4, 1997

The 4th of July in Europe just isn't the same, but we went to a barbeque put on by our program and did our best to make it so.

It was raining, and we got lost on the way. When we followed the directions to catch the bus, there was a bag over the schedule with the name of another stop on it. We took the alternate route on the sign and, like always, found our way eventually.

By the time we got to the barbeque, it had stopped raining but was still pretty cold – not like the 4th of July at all. The food was so good, though. The students bought or made all kinds of dishes. We got to have real chips and salsa for the first time in months and burgers with good old American cheese.

It was fun talking to everyone about the different experiences they've had and the people who have touched their lives. So many of us have grown so much through our time here.

When we left the celebration, there was that tug again. The odd feeling that I may never see most of those people again made the day bittersweet.

July 6, 1997

The moment has come when I am alone on the train to Basel, Switzerland, which will connect me to the night train to Paris. Everything I own is contained in two suitcases and my big backpack, and I'm again facing the unknown. I don't feel as scared this time – just regretful of everything I've left behind.

My wonderful semester is truly over now. I wish everything good didn't have to end. At least I'm "leaving while still having fun," as Dad told me on the phone before I left.

I'm still in shock that I'm really leaving and that things are officially over. I don't believe that I locked the door of Room 13 on the second story of *Merzhauserstraße* for the last time. I can't imagine that all the times I spent walking to and from the city center are over now. My room was so empty and lonely when I left, just like how I feel.

There was something about knowing there was always someone around to hang out with, to talk with, to dream with in any language you had in common. Never again will it be the same as it was when we were all together. Why did it have to end?

Being the first to go is difficult, but I guess it's better than being the last. I had to leave for Paris today to get the key from John before he leaves for the French Riviera. I might as well be leaving, though, because soon, being here won't be the same. Within a few days, pretty much everyone will be heading out.

Still, knowing it's all over is a feeling I've never quite felt before. I feel powerless to describe it in words. I'm letting go of a way of life that I'll never get back. While still desperately grasping for something I've left behind, I am embarking on something totally new.

My soon-to-be departure hung like a cloud over the whole day today. We went to the vineyards this afternoon but didn't stay long. Rain had been threatening the entire time I was packing, and it rolled in the moment we got there.

We were completely out in the open and got totally soaked. There was nothing we could do but laugh and dance in the rain. The unbridled joy of being together was a temporary reprieve from the heaviness of knowing that those moments were the last.

Hilda, Mark, Mike, Tom, Clarissa, and Anne rode to the train station to see me off. We all stuffed into Hilda's car, just like we'd done in that taxi in Basel. My overstuffed suitcases barely fit in the trunk. We laughed and made light conversation, as it was so difficult to face what was really happening.

On the platform at the station, I got to hug and share a moment with each one of them. Then I boarded the train at the last possible minute, finding a seat by the window. We exchanged one last wave as the train pulled away.

It's so sad and lonely sitting here now amidst all of these strangers chatting and laughing amongst themselves. For the first time since I embarked on this journey, no familiar faces are surrounding me.

July 7, 1997

It has been a long night with little sleep, on the same type of train I took with my friends when we went to Paris together. But this time, there was none of the same laughter and anticipation that I felt then. This time, there was only me and the unknown.

Through all my experiences, I know now that I am *capable* of fending for myself when I go to Paris. And I know that going to Paris is something I need to prove to myself on my own. Still, if I had the choice, I'd rather have my friends right here with me, headed on this next adventure.

As I travel further and further in the opposite direction, I long to jump off this train, put everything back in my apartment, and rewind it all back again…

Secrets from My Travel Diaries

> ➢ *It is easy to get so used to your surroundings that you forget how beautiful they are until you see them from afar.*

> ➢ *Leave while you're still having fun.*

> ➢ *Keep shining the light within you for the rest of your life.*

CHAPTER 21

My 30s: "You Can Have It All!"

"What exactly will make me happy?... Now more than ever,
I have no idea." - 1997

August 2, 2022

I draw myself back to the present day again. Yet, I still feel like I'm back in those vineyards in Freiburg, wondering once again who I am and what is true.

It's dawn, and the day is just starting to unfold. I take a deep breath. As if at the top of a wave, I hold my breath and then slowly let it out, exhaling all the noise. . . The distraction. . . The pain. . . The things I was sure were true. . .

. . . But are they?

Lately, I've been taking the time to notice the rising and setting of the sun instead of racing past them. On some brilliant days, the sun paints an entire color palette across the sky. Other days, it casts the sky in a vibrant orange, or a deep pink, or a fiery red.

Sometimes, it glides quietly over the horizon with little fanfare, as if slipping in and out the back door. And still others, it rises and sets behind thick clouds, doing what it does, even when I cannot see.

I guess life has cycles like that, too. . .

As I reflect on the sunrises and sunsets of my life, my thoughts travel to my 30s. I guess that's when, without realizing it, my objectives shifted from *"You can do it all"* to *"You Can Have It All."*

I had just turned 30 when I walked into a wine bar and met my husband. He was sitting at the bar, our eyes met, and everything played in slow motion. Feeling as though I was walking into an alternate universe, I sat down at the barstool next to him as if I was meant to be there all along. We stayed and talked for hours that first night.

As I advanced in my career, I had other focuses too – like getting married and my mom's health. Around the time I got engaged, my mom was diagnosed with pancreatic cancer. Her cancer was operable, but after the surgery, there were still traces in her lymph nodes. They spread aggressively, despite the rigorous chemo treatments.

I spent the next couple of years flying to see her as often as possible. Every moment was both precious and arduous.

Just before my wedding, I was selected for an international assignment. Going overseas was what I'd always dreamed of, but the circumstances surrounding it weren't the seamless flow of my dreams. My new husband's business and family were rooted in Houston. Meanwhile, my mom's health was still failing.

"You can have it all" was put to the test, and I knew this time I could not. I turned down the assignment. There would be another chance.

Shortly after my mom passed away, when I was already expecting our first child, that chance came. The start date of that assignment, and my due date, according to the ultrasound, coincided almost to the day. Again, the opportunity slid away into the horizon.

The early days as a family of three were so blissful. I believe we did "have it all" then. She was delightful and easygoing; we traveled with her everywhere. She loved the motion of going places and would fall asleep on planes and car rides. At the end of one flight, the man next to me said she'd been so peaceful under the blanket, that he hadn't even realized she was there (!).

Life was sheer bliss, the days full of unbridled joy. It felt like heaven, waking up with her sleeping peacefully in her bassinet beside me. By three months old, she was sleeping from seven o'clock at night until seven o'clock in the morning and taking two naps a day.

Our routine was flowing along nicely by the time she was five months old, which was when I had arranged to go back to work. I returned to a new role that kept me where I was geographically but was fulfilling and supported our lifestyle.

Life was a little more complicated but, overall, blissful and straightforward. I kept climbing the ladder at work, began traveling overseas again, and felt like I was in control of my life – at least most of the time.

After the birth of our son, almost three years later, the tides began to turn as the complexity factor increased. I took another five months off but was unable to get things back to flowing like before.

I doubled down on "*You Can Have It All,*" plunging in anyway, and returning to an intense role at work. This was where "having it all" began to bury me, like the avalanche at the Matterhorn.

Still, I could not let myself stop. I could only keep climbing.

Living and working downtown, I continued to take the city bus to the office. I remember one morning, it was early in the morning, still dark. I was on the bus in my suit and heels, exhausted. . . lost. I felt weighed down. . . heavy.

A man was sitting across from me on the bus, holding a large bouquet of red roses in his lap. He had been watching me intently, with care and concern. I looked down to avoid his eyes watching me.

His hair was matted, his clothes filthy, his skin dirty and creased. He looked rough, like he'd been living on the streets for a long time.

When I signaled for my stop, he stood up and stepped toward me, pulling a single red rose from the bouquet he was carrying. Standing face to face, his shining eyes seemed to see through me and pierce my soul.

He held the rose out to me.

At that moment, his rough exterior fell away, and he looked like an angel. I would never have thought he "had it all," but I knew he possessed something that I did not.

In a fog, my legs carried me into the office, still clutching his rose in my hand.

"When I look in the mirror, I no longer know who I see..."

I didn't understand what that ache was that I felt on the bus that day. But somewhere amid the vast array of colorful pictures in my camera roll, I had put "you can have it all" at the helm of my life.

And I was trying to "have it all" by "doing it all," but "having" and "doing" are two very different things. "Doing" is tangible. It can be divided up into tasks and milestones. I was good at "doing."

"I do know that I want to live! Not just be alive. I don't want to become so over-ambitious that I forget that. I know I have the natural tendency to push myself to the limit."

But "having" requires something different entirely. It requires slowing down and taking the time to go deeper. . . to develop relationships and share the moments that don't make the "to-do" list. It doesn't always follow a schedule.

Meanwhile, in all the "doing" to get the "having," I was barely able to get my head above water. The questions I forgot I'd written in 1997 resurfaced to answer yet again.

"What exactly will make me happy? What kind of life... career... man... will light a fire inside me that will keep me going each day for the rest of my life? What kind of career can show me the world but still allow me to develop roots that will be lasting? Now more than ever, I have no idea."

I had answered the question once and got exactly what I said I wanted, but I didn't recognize it. I didn't know it, and it didn't look like I thought, because "all" is not a destination. It is infinite. . . undefined.

"All" is always on the horizon and receding further and further away. Pursuing "all" had left me with a wistful feeling in the undercurrents of my subconscious. Deep down, I knew that instead of "all," there was something. . . more.

Yet I was at the exact cross-rounds I had written about in those long-forgotten diaries that had been hidden in the box above my business suits.

"I have a feeling there must be something I was put on this earth to do, and I wonder now if I really do want to go into business or something else entirely."

Amid everything that I felt I "should," I'd pushed down what was in my heart.

... But what is in my heart?

I pack up and rise to my feet, legs stiff from sitting for so long. The aches and pains leave my body as I feel reignited and alive with the thought of finding fresh answers.

It is time to travel back into the "frozen-in-time" pages of my diary, to go back and rediscover. . .

Paris.

Secrets from My Travel Diaries

➤ *The sun is still shining, even when you can't see it.*

➤ *Instead of "all," there is something. . . more.*

➤ *The tides of routine are strong; break free and find out what you are here to do.*

Zermatt

Our Bahn to the Matterhorn

The Matterhorn

Near the
Matterhorn

Rothenburg o.d. Tauber?
No- Tübingen am
Neckar
May 7, 1997

The Tübingen Wave

Prost to
Tübingen

May 8 - Sound of Music Tour
in Salzburg, Austria

The Sound of Music Gazebo

The Sound of Music

Let's Sing!

The Graveyard

Botanical Gardens –
München
Rathaus

München
you aren't sick on
your birthday are you?
(Nice hair)

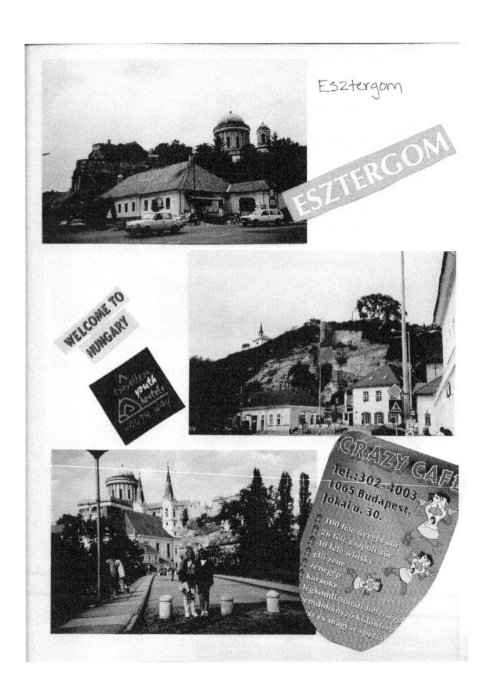

Flowers for oil...
Man, how tall are
those things?

Stenshuvud

Sunset over Lund

Look at those KΔ's!

Copenhagen-

My vineyard

An end of the semester drink at the Bier Garten above Freiburg. Mmm... Hefe weißen

Snow Flakes and choc Blops

PART 3

WHERE TRAVEL IS LIGHT

CHAPTER 22

Pounding the Pavement – Parisian Style

"I've gone through so many ups and downs since I came to Paris. I guess this is to be expected because I'm doing this completely on my own, knowing no one in the city, having to figure everything out for myself."

July 7, 1997

I woke up on the train to the sun rising over the outskirts of Paris, and it filled me with nervous excitement. Then, I passed by so many tourist attractions in the taxi to John's apartment and felt another surge of, "I'm really making this happen!"

John met me here briefly to give me the keys. Now I'm here in this apartment, feeling utterly exhausted and more alone than I've ever felt in my life.

I'm feeling those tugs in two different directions again. Part of me just wants to go home now and forget this whole thing. Another part of me is excited to see what's around the corner.

Coming here means stepping out on my own like never before. Here, there is no program, no itinerary, and no Clarissa, Anne, Mike, or Tom. There is just a small office with some job connections and a short-term student visa. The rest is up to me. It's exciting and scary at the same time.

In junior high school French class, the seed of this dream was planted. The teacher brought in a camera, and we filmed role plays about working in a café in Paris. I saw myself in that dream, leaning in to take an order and serve my customers. Now, I'm here to chase it, to move through fear and create something on my own. And I'm here to work on my French.

Depending on how things work out, I'll stay about a month just while I have this apartment. If an internship with John's company works out, I may stay longer. But no matter what, I'm working in that café and going back to Germany to visit before going home. I'm ahead on my credits and don't have to rush back for the semester.

I feel so scared, though – I just want to retreat to what I know. Nothing makes sense anymore.

Everything is a risk, though… Every new thing requires a little fear.

Surely, things will get better. I am so incredibly tired. After some sleep, I'll figure things out and get organized…

July 8, 1997

John said that he usually works all day and goes out all evening, using this apartment mainly as a crash pad. I guess that's why it's so basic.

In the main room, there is a closet, a desk that looks more like a workbench and takes up most of the room, and a couple of stools. There is no curtain on the window, no place to sit and eat, and no TV – nothing but a small clock radio.

On one side of the main room, there is a small kitchen. It's equipped with a pot, a pan, a few pieces of silverware, and a few dishes. In the bedroom, the bed and small table take up the entire room. The electricity only works in the bedroom and in the toilet.

The best thing about this apartment are the large windows that stretch across the bedroom wall. When I open those windows, the excitement of Paris fills this boring place from below. Outside my window, the Eiffel Tower stands there majestically, shining on me at night.

It's so lonely here, though. Sitting in this apartment, I can't help asking myself why I left everything I've ever known to come here.

I slept through the morning today. I've been feeling so run down from the end-of-semester rush and the sporadic snatches of sleep on the train.

This afternoon, I went to the program office to check out the job postings. I met a guy at the program office, and he said that he had been camping out between the office's four walls for over a month, trying to find a decent job. I'm realizing it is going to take some major work to line something up here. Somehow, I will do it.

After one last look at the Eiffel Tower, lit up from my bedroom window, I will turn out the light...

July 9, 1997

I made some calls this morning, and one person is calling me back, but the others just want me to send a cover letter and resume. The thought of going to the program office to customize cover letters for each employer just exhausts me.

I keep feeling like I just want to be back in Freiburg again. It's so overwhelming to be alone in this huge city. I have to keep reminding myself that things wouldn't be the same in Freiburg, either, because no one is there anymore.

I know something will turn up here; I'm just terrible at waiting for things.

Even though I feel the squeeze of running out of money, I went out today to do some shopping. The second I stepped off the train to Paris, my wardrobe became even more wrong than it sometimes was in the places I traveled.

People get a lot more dressed up here, and if I want to find a job, I'd better look my best. Unfortunately, anything I'd need is sitting in my closet at home. It's not that I'm all that chic there, either, but at least I have something beyond the white tennis shoes, jeans, and T-shirts in my suitcases.

After looking everywhere, I finally went back and bought the red dress I'd seen in one of the first shops I went to. The saleslady was the only one who gave me the time of day in all that shopping.

Already, Freiburg feels like it was an eternity ago. My last days there feel like they were from another life I've already left behind in this whirlwind of changing lives. I just wish I knew what to do. This is such a big step on my own.

I knew things would be rocky at first, though. Maybe I just need a little time to search for myself, find the confidence within, and all that. Maybe then I can move forward. I thought I would lose it, sitting in the program office, trying to force myself to write a cover letter. I have to pull myself together and realize this is all part of the adventure.

July 10, 1997

This afternoon, I hit the pavement after *Mittagspause* [German for "lunch break"], or whatever they call it here. Looking for any "Help Wanted" signs I could find, I walked the streets and found one restaurant that seemed promising. It's called *Le Tex-Mex*.

Though not exactly the French café in my dream, it's an advantage to be an American there, and I'll take whatever advantage I can get. There is so much competition for jobs here.

I went in to speak with the manager, and we sat together on the stools at the bar. He asked me why I wanted to work there, and I confidently told him that it was my dream to work at a café in Paris. He looked intrigued and said, *"Ton reve peut realiser."* ["Your dream may come true."] Then, after the interview, he let me order whatever I wanted from the menu for lunch.

After that, I went to a few other restaurants and talked to the managers. American restaurants seem to be the best bet to get a job. TGI Fridays offered me a chance to be a bus girl, but I really want to hold out for a waitress job.

July 10, 1997, 5 PM

I'm sitting on a bench in the middle of the *Jardin de Luxembourg* feeling frustrated and in total despair. (This, of course, makes me even madder at myself for becoming frustrated so easily!)

I went into a store with a sign outside saying they were looking for a salesperson, even though I knew the place was fancy and probably out of my league. When the manager walked up to me to talk about the job, I froze up, and some unintelligible babble came out of my mouth.

As I stood there mortified, he totally shot me down, ranting that I don't speak French well enough to be employed there and looking offended that I'd even come in. Honestly, I understand where he was coming from, which only served to add to my frustration.

Where is that confidence within, anyway? I need to find someone to practice speaking French with. I still have too much German in my head and can never seem to spit things out.

I wonder what these coming weeks will bring. There are so many ups and downs right now. I hate this solitude, and I have a security issue because I have no one to walk home with. Guys keep coming up and talking to me. When I was walking back from the Metro, it was getting dark, and this group of guys were making comments to me. I ignored them, and they started swearing at me.

I know I need to make things happen for myself, but I'm surrounded by strangers everywhere, with no idea who to trust. I'm longing for the ease with which I was able to meet people to hang out with in Freiburg.

Sometimes I feel really good about things, then I plummet, and then I'm stable again. I'm just so confused about what to do. Of course, this is normal, though, because I've only been here for a few days.

I keep finding myself trying to speak German to people everywhere, too. I don't think it's clicked yet that I'm not in Germany anymore. Maybe I just need to take some time to step back from this running around and realize that I'm in France. Then maybe I'll be able to figure out what I can do to make it in this city.

Every time I've been to Paris, I've had a totally different impression of it, as if it were a new place. The first time I was here at 16, I was overwhelmed by the mere fact that I was seeing everything I'd memorized for the Paris unit in French class.

When I came here a few months ago for the third time, we were dragged everywhere by Mike and Tom's friends. It was tiring but great because I was among friends that meant everything to me, and adventure seemed to follow us everywhere.

This time I'm not quite sure what impression I have of the city yet. I do know that it's completely different from when I was traveling. Suddenly, I'm not in line to go up the *Arc de Triomphe*. Instead, I'm taking the *Metro* from one place to another, combing the city for jobs with a resume in hand.

I imagine there will be parts of the city that I'll come to love like there were in Freiburg. They will not necessarily be where tourists would ever set foot, either. It's just that I haven't found those places yet…

July 11, 1997

Today started bad and got worse. I got off the *Metro* on the opposite side of the street from the address I wanted and had to walk a long way back. When I finally got to the right place, I found that the restaurant didn't open until four o'clock in the afternoon.

Then I went to another restaurant that was supposedly hiring. It turned out I had the wrong location. I'll have to try again tomorrow to find the right one.

I wore the new sandals I'd bought to look nice for the employers and walked around the city until my feet felt like they were going to fall off. Unfortunately, I didn't find much of anything promising available.

On the way back, I went down the street to the grocery store. I bought the cheapest food I could find and made a successful meal with the one pot in the kitchen.

July 12, 1997

I'm sitting here on a lonely Saturday night in Paris. During parts of today, I felt worse than ever. I read a little bit of my diary about my adventures in Freiburg and felt a lot better about things. It helped me remember that I do have friends – it's just that they're not here.

Sometimes, all I want to do is cry to Mom or call the airline and see if I could get back to the U.S. ASAP. I feel desperate, like I have nowhere to turn and no one I can count on. I miss being at home terribly and can't even remember anymore how it felt to have what I have there.

It would be such a cop-out if I left, though. I want nothing more than to jet out of here right now, but I have to stay and see what happens.

July 13, 1997

My mood has plummeted again to the depths of despair. I'm here at the park, trying to read a book John recommended so that I can try and improve my French.

I'm finding it so hard to get into reading, though. This bench is so uncomfortable, and everyone walking by is so interesting. There's been music playing all day, advertising an outdoor concert. I'd love to go, but I wouldn't want to deal with going alone.

When I look around, no one is alone but me. Everyone else is either walking hand in hand with a significant other or chatting with friends or family members.

I had a nightmare last night that my friends died in a car crash, and I was running around through the remnants of the explosion, trying desperately to find them. I guess for me it's as if all my friends are gone now, though (thank goodness) they are still alive, as far as I know. It seems so strange to be separated after being together all the time for so long.

All throughout this week, it was all I could do to keep my spirits up enough to look for opportunities. All I wanted to be able to do was take a day off and not deal with any of it. But now that the weekend is here, I dread the long day with no busyness to escape to.

The days since my arrival here seem to be sliding by, and sometimes I wonder what I'm even doing. I'm learning a lot just from being here – that much is for sure. It just feels like I've had so much confusion.

I'm torturing myself about what I'm going to do to get a job here. I have to stop thinking about it and just accept what is. It's just so difficult right now. I'm fighting with myself all the time.

July 14, 1997

I took myself to the Bastille Day parade today. It felt like a lot of standing around in the crowds, waiting for something to happen. Finally, a bunch of good-looking military men appeared in tanks. Jets thundered overhead, giving off red, white, and blue smoke, followed by the appearance of President Jacques Chirac.

Back at my apartment, I'm watching the fireworks over the Eiffel Tower from my bedroom window. It is difficult to describe the feeling of standing on my bed with my window opened to the world, the wind racing across my face, and the Eiffel Tower shining outside. How lucky I am to be able to experience this at any moment I choose!

July 15, 1997

At the program office, I found another interesting job ad. It was from a woman looking for a native English speaker, 18 to 24 years old, to travel with her and look after her six-year-old daughter. The hiring contract would be for two months, and everything would be paid for – food, housing, and travel expenses, plus 1,200 francs (about $200) per month.

I talked to the lady about the job and arranged to meet at her house. She interviewed me and then had me clean a room in her house as a "*petit test.*" (The French seem to be big on these.)

She asked me to call her at the end of the month so that I could set up a time to play with her kid for an hour. Then, she'd decide if I got the job or not.

It didn't sound too promising, though, because she said she was interviewing about 30 people. Inevitably, at least one of them has probably already been an au pair and knows exactly what to do. So much for that idea.

After the "*petit test,*" I missed the *Metro* by a couple of seconds and had to wait for what felt like forever for another one to arrive. Then, I went out of the way to pick up the film I had dropped off to be developed, but they said it wouldn't be ready until tomorrow.

With aching, blistered feet from wearing my new sandals, I finally got back to the apartment. There, I somehow proceeded to burn my food. I tried to eat it anyway, but between the burned flavor and not liking the taste of the seasoning I'd used, I finally declared it inedible.

At this point, I am more than a little ready to read for a while – and close the book on today.

July 16, 1997

I was at the program office writing down some job listings this afternoon when one of the ladies working there came over very rudely and informed me that they were closed. She kept repeating over and over again in both French and English in a condescending way as if I was someone off the streets who needed to be shooed away.

I couldn't help crying as I left. I want to be strong, but I'm having so much trouble handling anything right now. I have absolutely no support here. I keep feeling that I just want to go home, but my own personal pride makes me stay. Oh, how I hate all this.

July 17, 1997

I went to do another "*petit test*" for some freelance work, translating tourist brochures from French to English. Then, I got a call from *Le Tex-Mex* to go back for another interview (which ended up meaning working for free at the restaurant).

On the way there, I went to another restaurant that was hiring, called the Indian Cafe, just for good measure. I cut it closer than I should have to get to *Le Tex-Mex* because part of the *Metro* was under construction, which confused me.

Instead of an interview, that "*petit test*" turned out to be a full night of work. Another newly hired waitress named Andrea, who is from Texas, showed me the ropes. (That was nice because that way, I didn't have to deal with learning it all in French.) The time flew by, as I really enjoyed the people working there and liked serving the customers at the restaurant.

The whole night I also felt nervous about whether I'd be given the job. In the end, the manager called me *tu* [the informal "you"] (which hopefully is a good sign) and told me he'd call next week.

July 18, 1997

All at once, I feel like I just can't take it anymore. I've had enough of all of this. The longer I stay shut up in this apartment, the more depressed I become.

I'm so scared of running out of money, and I have no idea what I would do if I did. I have almost nothing left of what I've saved anymore. Why does money take so long to earn and then erodes away so quickly?

I'm sick of passing by places I can't afford to go, with friends that I don't have – and can't meet because everything costs money. I feel like someone who's been away from home too long, is trying to do too much, and has no money left to enjoy the country she's in any longer.

I have no more energy to run around looking for a job – especially because I know I won't get one since I have no interest in staying here any longer.

All I want to do is go home.

I want to go out to breakfast with my dad and cook dinner with my mom.

I want to go to a big mall and say, "Thank you" to the salesperson and receive a smile and a reply in an American accent in return.

I want to go back to school, sing "Friends in Low Places," and drink Coors Light with my friends.

I want to go to a bar where I have to wear a "21" band so I can drink a beer.

I want to drive down the road in my car, sing to the radio, and pull into a Taco Bell.

I want to see if the attendant at the gas station still remembers my name.

I want to find some nice American guy who I can really relate to – even if it's just me and my friend Tyler, getting sloshed on cheap beer on the ripped, smelly couches of the football house.

And I want to see if any of the guys I thought I could date before I left are real possibilities or just a fleeting thought because I knew I was leaving.

I want to visit my brother at college and see how he's doing there.

I want to take my photo album to show my parents, my relatives, and my friends.

I want to tell them all about my adventures and say things like, "Oh, to be a student in Europe again …" for the rest of my life.

Suddenly, I'm craving chicken parmesan and nachos.

Just give me my car, a nice American guy, the people I love, and everything so familiar since the day I was born.

And give me the chance to show the people at home how much they mean to me!

I've had enough of Europe – something I never thought I would say.

I'm tired of waiting.

I'm tired of just about everything.

I've learned so much about myself, and now I'm done.

Just put me on a plane and ship me home!

Secrets from My Travel Diaries

> ➢ *Perseverance and determination are the ticket to your dreams.*

> ➢ *Things don't necessarily happen on your timeline or look exactly as you imagine them.*

> ➢ *Give yourself grace – and permission to rant – once in a while.*

CHAPTER 23

Eiffel Tower, My Guardian Angel

"The Eiffel Tower is like my guardian angel. It helps orient me in the city, presides over the park where I like to go, and shines on me at night through my window."

July 19, 1997

I'm feeling much better than I did yesterday, sitting here in what I've decided is my favorite part of Paris: *Le Champs de Mars,* the garden where the Eiffel Tower stands at the far end.

Earlier, I walked over to the Eiffel Tower and stood underneath, just as I did nearly five years ago to the day when I visited Europe for the first time. I had forgotten how it feels to stand underneath it and look up. Something caught in my throat as I stood there, taking in that perspective, as everyone around me just walked on by.

The Eiffel Tower must have seen so much presiding over this city. I love looking for it all over Paris. It prevails majestically over the bustle of people strolling through the park, the Parisians honking down the streets, and the tourists floating down the Seine.

As I sit alone on this park bench, I'm surrounded by tourists. They are chattering, eating ice cream, and shelling out top dollar (or *franc*) to go up the Eiffel Tower. All around me, little kids from all over the world are pouting, running, and yelling in their mother tongues; I don't think they even know that they are in another country.

After seeing the sights that everyone sees, most of these tourists will be gone in the blink of an eye. The next time I come here, they will already be in some other part of the continent or even the world.

In some ways, I'd like to be in their shoes – it's so much easier. But I also know that the tourist experience only captures a small part of the pulsating vibe of Paris. Life outside of the tourist attractions is what I have the unique opportunity to discover. When these tourists are long gone, I will still be here, living and learning day by day.

It's finally hitting me that I actually have done what I set out to do. I have a place of residence here that is not a hotel, and I officially have a job!

When I reported on *Le Tex-Mex* yesterday afternoon, I wore my new dress and arrived early to have dinner first, as the manager, Jean, instructed. He and I sat together at the bar while I ate enchiladas with rice and beans, and he gave me the scoop. They were having two private parties, one upstairs and one downstairs. He said I'd have to stay until both were over – probably until at least five o'clock in the morning.

I worked hard serving food and drinks for a couple of hours downstairs. Then, when we finished, I went upstairs to the other party. There was a band playing, with people dancing everywhere. I just stood there with the rest of the staff for a while because there was nothing specific to do. Then the managers, followed by everyone else, started intermixing with the party and dancing on top of the bar.

The party didn't break up until about six o'clock in the morning, and we had to stay and clean up, putting tables back and things like that. Afterward, we all stayed for breakfast *quesadillas*.

July 21, 1997

All at once, things are happening. I got a call from John, saying that he'd gotten me an "in" for a position at his company. Apparently, the international manager, Antoine, mentioned that someone was about to go on maternity leave, and they have no one to replace her.

John told Antoine about me and gave me his contact information. I called and set up an interview for the next day. Then, I spent the rest of the day rehearsing a summary of my background and previous internships so that I could talk fluently in French about them.

After the interview, Antoine turned me over to Celine, who was going on leave. She immediately started training me as if it had already been decided that I would take the position. I was escorted back to Antoine's office and was sipping a Perrier when he came back in and told me that Celine gave me a good recommendation.

He told me he wanted to hire me, but Celine wasn't returning for six months, and I needed to be available until then. This completely shook me because of the ripple effect to my plans.

Staying that long would mean missing part of the spring semester and not graduating with my class. I'd also need to figure out an extension of my work visa, because mine is valid for a maximum of three months. And I'd have to find another apartment.

Antoine said he'd call me to let me know the next steps, reiterating that he needs to fill the position quickly.

I feel so torn. I love being spontaneous when it comes to some things, but when it comes to life decisions, I just hate not knowing. There are certain things that, as much as I might want to change, I feel like I've made little progress. Wanting to feel in control of my life is one of them. Maybe it's just the way I am. I don't know.

Before now, my life through the years of school was always so organized and structured. Now I'm faced with so many choices. Part of me longs for the stability of the past, while another part is excited about the future stretching out before me.

There are always two sides to everything, pulling me in different directions. Once again, the world feels like a confusing, unpredictable place.

July 22, 1997

There was a handwritten paper pinned to the board at the program office advertising an apartment at a good price. I called the number and arranged to check it out.

It turns out the price is so low because it's extremely cramped, and there is only one bed and a foldout couch among the three of us who would be living there. There is also only one key, so I'd have to leave it in the mailbox when I went out. It's nice that it's so cheap, but. . .

Mom and Dad are getting worried. They said they are going to call again in a couple of days to find out what is going on in my life. I just don't know what to do.

Even the *Champs de Mars* was no sanctuary for me today. A guy sat down on my bench and was aggressive, bothering me and telling me he was in love with me. I managed to get away from him, taking a different way back to my apartment so he wouldn't know where I lived. As usual, I went the wrong way, and got lost. I had to retrace my steps and finally got back, thankfully, without seeing him again.

I feel like I have no clue where to turn – even more so than I did before. I am increasingly aware that there is no one I can count on in this city. There is no one to cry to for help, or pick up the pieces for me, or pull me out of somewhere I don't want to be. I feel fear welling up inside me every time I think of being in a situation from which I can't escape.

July 23, 1997

There have been so many ups and downs here. However, I feel like, at least now, I am able to communicate more freely in French and seem to have overcome the initial difficulties of switching from German.

I went out a couple of times with Julien, who I met at *Le Tex-Mex*. He took me out to a quaint café, and we spoke French the whole time, exchanging ideas on life in France and the U.S.

It was a lot of fun because I've always wanted to go to a place like that in Paris and have never been able to afford it. I liked getting dressed up and going on a real date in Paris. It's a far cry from putting on a pair of jeans and a T-shirt and hanging out over a couple of beers at school. Then again, I never went out with anyone who wasn't a student until I came to Europe, so I can't really compare.

Julien did what I've always seen in the movies: he asked me what I liked, added some other things for me to try, and ordered for both of us. I didn't even know what was arriving until it was placed in front of me. It was all served in small portions, and more kept coming every time I thought we'd received everything.

Afterward, we walked down the Champs-Elysées and then went swing dancing. I had a great time and caught on pretty quickly with him leading, but I still felt like an amateur compared to everyone else. When we took a break, it was fun just watching everyone dancing with such energy, all dressed up like the Parisians usually are.

By the end of the evening, I felt a feeling of unease, though. Julien kept coming on too strong… making comments… inviting me to join him on vacation, all expenses paid…

There was a haunting sort of underlying inner unhappiness about him. . . an emptiness that he's looking to fill. It scared me a little. And I know that I'm not the one to fill it.

It feels like I've pinched pennies for so long, and I'm so tired of it. It was so freeing to be wined and dined – and to have someone to be with. That is the lure of wanting to keep going with him, even though deep down I don't feel right about it. . .

Later, I called and confided in Mom about it. I told her how he had taken me out and promised me the world without me having to pay for anything. "But at what cost to you?" she asked me pointedly.

I can't get those words out of my head now. I guess I always thought of cost as monetary. But there is a cost, deeper than money, that I never understood before. It's something else that has value. That something is *me*.

All at once, I realize I'd rather sit alone in this apartment, eating my 12-franc muesli with my 3-franc milk, than dine on a gourmet dinner and compromise myself. There are some things that money can't buy.

July 24, 1997

Andrea and I had a really good talk today. I really admire her. She's been in Paris for two years, speaks very good French, seems so sophisticated, and really knows the ins and outs.

It's only through sheer determination that she's been able to stay afloat, though. She eventually got a job, but spent about a month with so little money left that she could only afford to eat half a baguette per day.

Hearing that shocked me. I've been so worried about money, but I also know that my family has been like my anchor, protecting me even from afar. Even though I am alone here, I am not without support. She doesn't have that kind of support.

Though we come from different backgrounds, her story really made me think. I guess I'm just one of many who have come to Paris, looking for something and struggling to find it. I came to Paris, imagining the movies where people come here and meet the loves of their lives or change dramatically into someone totally different.

Life is not the movies, though. It is not all dazzling glamor like I once thought. Along with the light, there is a dark side – a struggle going on behind the scenes, a desperation to do what it takes to survive. Now, I even feel like I can see those men who robbed us in Budapest in a different light.

Because I've stayed here longer, I've seen some of the good and the bad that dwell below the surface. It's so much clearer than if you just travel for a short period of time and see a handful of sites through rose-colored glasses. I'm not so charmed by absolutely everything anymore.

I can't say that I really understand how this complicated world works yet. However, there are certain universals that, with the experience I've gained,

I'm starting to see as patterns. I guess that fits in exactly with my theory that there are two sides to everything when you look below the surface.

I'm realizing some dreams aren't quite what they seem, either – like my fascination with becoming a waitress in Paris. It sounded so romantic, and it is fun, but ultimately, I'd definitely rather have a business career.

What chasing that dream has really given me, though, is confidence and gratitude. I have found confidence within myself, and I've realized that I don't need to get it from anyone else.

I've also learned to appreciate how much it means to have a family who loves and supports me – even if they're far away. With them, there is a feeling of unity, protection, and comfortable interdependence that is different from anything else. Now that I have been without them, I know there is nothing and no one who can replace them.

I feel so free now because I know I've unlocked so many things I never knew. I'm so much more capable than I ever realized: of loving and being loved and telling the people who mean everything just how much they mean.

July 25, 1997

Someone called from Antoine's office a few days ago, asking me what kind of visa I had. I know they are still working on filling the position. John told me that Antoine would be calling me today, so I stayed at my apartment all afternoon, reading a book and waiting for his call.

It's getting to be evening now, and I'm still sitting here waiting. I hate it, but I have no choice. No one ever seems to call unless I'm out or rushing off somewhere, and there's no answering machine to know who called.

Being stuck in this apartment for so long is driving me insane. What in the world is taking him so long? Probably he's already found someone else and is just hoping I'll go away or disappear so he doesn't have to break the news to me. What he doesn't understand, though, is that I no longer care. I'd rather just know and not wait any longer.

I talked to Mom, and she made me feel so much better. She told me what I needed to hear and helped me find direction. Most importantly, she reminded me that I have nothing to prove here and should just be having fun in France. This made me realize that I've been so concerned about money and finding work that I forgot what matters. I've been given this opportunity to be here and need to make the most of it.

I finally went ahead and called Antoine myself. He said that he couldn't give me the job for legal reasons, even though he seemed sincere about wanting to. I understand he needs someone for more than three months, and I don't have the right work visa. More than anything now, though, I just feel relieved just to be moving on.

All throughout the day today, I kept catching glimpses of the Eiffel Tower out my window. It seemed to me like a guardian angel watching over me. I love looking at it from afar, at the way it casts its light on the city below, making Paris look like a fairyland. Yet I've also learned that it's only when you get up close that you can see what's really there.

Secrets from My Travel Diaries

➢ *When you get caught up in doing, it's easy to forget what matters.*

➢ *Value isn't only about money; you have value, too.*

➢ *Stepping out to live your dreams builds confidence and gratitude.*

CHAPTER 24

Am I Already... Here?

*"I see now that I've already become the person that I aspired
to be – and done the things that I aspired to do..."*

July 26, 1997

Once again, I'm confused, just when I'd already made my decision. I received
a call from the manager of the New York Muffin Company, where I'd left my
CV. She was super nice and offered me a job on the spot. She wants me to
work there for three months, starting in a few weeks.

It's tempting to stay, and I don't need the fall semester to graduate in the
spring. Still, I know it was one thing to stay here for a professional role, and
another to spend the next three months selling muffins.

I called Mom and told her about it.

Around midnight I was just about to go to bed when Dad called unexpectedly.
He is disgusted that after all my education, I've been working as a waitress and
cleaning people's houses as a "test." I really wanted to learn French, but this is
becoming ridiculous.

Dad's advice was to have fun, go to London like I wanted, and visit my host families in Germany. Then, when the summer ends, he said I should just come home. He's lined up an internship for me, which I guess people are clamoring for. I know I'll lose it if I don't get back to the U.S. in time.

On the phone with him, I realized that I must have been crazy to think I should stay here and sell muffins when I could be with the people I love, building my international career. Perhaps now, I'm finally coming to my senses.

Now that I'm off the phone, I feel a strange sense of loss, though. On the one hand, I'm relieved. This gives me a sort of permission to move on because I've already done what I came here to do. But I also feel an underlying disappointment. He always told me that I could do anything, but now I see that there were limitations…

After our conversation, I couldn't sleep a wink. I finally turned on the radio at around three o'clock in the morning. Two different versions of *Brown Eyed Girl* – one of my all-time favorite songs – came on the radio within minutes. I took it as a sign to just be happy, danced around the room, and sang along.

Then, I started planning my travels.

I know now that I have been so truly blessed. From this experience, I have learned that things have a way of working out, whether you bother to stress about them or not.

I've been making myself miserable, thinking of my stay in Europe ending, as much as I want to be back with my family and friends at home. And I've felt so much pressure to do absolutely everything I ever wanted to do. But I'm starting to realize that those feelings stemmed from the thought of working for decades without ever having an opportunity to do something like this again.

So many people don't decide what they really want to do until they're middle-aged. Surely, I still have time. I know now that I still have other dreams to follow and truths to be learned.

Eventually, priorities change, and I imagine I will settle into a life of stability and a career. But before then, there is more that I need to do. And I know that if I want something badly enough, I will achieve it. I have proven that to myself in Paris.

It feels liberating to shed my worries and have direction in my life – at least for now. I feel like opening the window and shouting over the rooftops to the Eiffel Tower, "*I am free!*"

I am free – to bum around for a little while, to wander and enjoy being in Europe. And after this time of standing on my own, I'm free not to have to anymore. I'm free to go back to Germany and back home, graduate with my class, and have more adventures.

When I leave Paris, I will have no extra baggage and no international boo-boos. But, inside, I know Paris will have left her mark on me. Somehow, being here has changed me somehow, and I will never be quite the same again.

July 27, 1997

Today, I went to the *Champs-Elysées* to watch the end of the *Tour de France* with millions of other people. I enjoyed the big parade with floats by all the race sponsors. Then, I wandered down the street, watching all the people and peering between heads to see what was happening on the street.

After about two hours, the first cyclists came across the finish line. I got caught up in their incredible speed and the excitement for a while, but eventually got tired of the crowds and left.

Just as I was walking in the door to the apartment, Ryker called. I met him when I was with Andrea, and he gave me his phone number. Eons ago, before everything went down with the muffins, I called the number he gave me. It turned out to be his work number, and when he answered, he was in the middle of a meeting. He said he was happy I called, hadn't been sure I was going to, and would call me back.

Ironically, Ryker is the first person I've met who was actually born in Freiburg, Germany. He works in Paris and does something with computers for an American consulting company I haven't heard of. He seemed to be doing well financially but really enjoying his work, too.

Anyway, he did call back and invited me out for dinner. Something – I guess it was curiosity – made me say yes, even though I've already decided to move on in a few days. I enjoyed going out with him immensely.

We spoke mainly in English, with a little German and French mixed in. He speaks perfect English with virtually no accent.

It's been a long time since I've talked with someone about anything of any depth in English, and I've never had that kind of conversation with someone whose native tongue wasn't English. I guess I use a lot of expressions to convey what I'm thinking. I never thought about it until he had to keep asking me what things I was saying meant.

Ryker is so observant about many things that I never thought of before – perhaps because he's lived all over Europe and met people from all over the world. There is something about him – elusive, direct, yet impossible to understand. Something deeper, almost forbidden, about him draws me in.

It drove me crazy when he said, "There is something that we've both been looking for. Something about one another that we wanted to know more about. And that's why we're here."

He was so right. He said he saw me as someone who knew what she wanted but was still searching for herself and where she wanted to be long-term.

Something about the things he said and how he said them intrigued me as I had never felt before. He treats me very independently, more so than anyone I've ever met.

After dinner, when we were getting on the metro, I stepped back and let him lead without thinking about it. He immediately picked up on that and remarked that it "surprised" him. I guess I just do it naturally, but I've never had anyone question it.

On the way to the club, we ran into one of his French coworkers in the metro, and Ryker invited him along. That turned the conversation to French for the rest of the night – when we spoke at all, as it was very loud, and people were dancing everywhere.

Once at the club, Ryker became a loner, dancing by himself and buying us round after round of beers. He drank heavily but always seemed in control, like he knew exactly what he was doing. I spent most of the time hanging out with his colleague and was glad he was there.

When the bar closed, I was still wondering what to think. We got in a cab, and Ryker acted very aloof, saying he was going to another club down the road after dropping me off. Instead, we ended up standing outside my apartment forever, talking about all kinds of things.

There was a lone motorcycle parked on the street outside my apartment. He straddled it like he owned it, sitting on it as if it were a chair. The street was deserted. Things began to get heavy, and eventually, he left, leaving me wondering who he really was.

I've never met anyone like him. He's a good-looking guy, but the world has lots of those. There was something different about how he piqued my curiosity.

August 1, 1997

I haven't heard from Ryker, and I've decided I'm over it. Perhaps he is meant to remain a mystery to me. He's the kind of guy that could get under my skin if I let him. The "rational me" says that's not what I want to put myself through right now.

Not hearing from him makes it so much easier – it's hard enough to leave as it is.
I went for a walk this morning, and even if I hadn't known the date, it would have been obvious. August has hit, and with it, the departure of what seems to be every Parisian in the city.

Along with the throngs of people exiting the city, I know it's time for me to leave too. I've done all that I set out to do.

It breaks my heart to think of leaving, but I feel like I did the last day in Freiburg: If I have to leave, I just want to get it over with instead of hanging around.

It was downright depressing walking down the street. It was lined with people packing their cars and leaving in droves. I feel like I'm seeing only tourists here now.

Walking to the *Champs de Mars* made me even more depressed. They are tearing up the entire garden – maybe because no Parisians are left to complain.

It's not helping my mood that today is so foggy that I can hardly make out the Eiffel Tower from my window. It's as if even the city is covered in misery over the sudden loss of all its inhabitants. Nobody is familiar anymore – just crowds of people from different corners of the earth who want to see a little bit of Paris, even without all the Parisians.

I was reading the diary entry I wrote when I was sitting on my balcony only a few days into my stay in Germany. I had so many hopes and dreams about how things would be and what I would learn.

I wanted to:
- meet German friends and people all over the world.
- have at least one brief fling.
- "really" make it on my own in Paris.
- work on my German and French.
- "make the right decisions and continue to follow my dreams."

When I look at that list, I know that I've succeeded in accomplishing every one of the things I dreamed of. In fact, I've done far more.

When I left Freiburg at the end of the semester, I had collected the right materials to build what I wanted and had begun piecing it together. But it's been in Paris that I've begun to really get clarity on who I am and how much I've changed. And it's here that I've learned that not only can I make it on my own, but I can actually enjoy doing it, too.

Sometimes I've felt lost in the crowd of millions of people carrying out their daily lives, a part in which I have no role. But living in a big city with so much going on has also been so exciting. I feel such a kinship with this place. Paris has been my own experience to discover – from the days I spent miserable and alone, to my triumph of turning things around and making the experience my own.

When I first met Andrea, I saw her as an independent person – someone who seemed to know so much about how the world works. I thought she was the kind of person I could someday become. But I see now that, in many ways, I've already become the person I aspired to be.

I'm doing what I've always wanted to do and meeting people from all over the world. I really feel that I grew up here in Europe – the rest of the way, anyway. Being here has helped me realize what I'm capable of. And Europe has also helped me appreciate the people in this world who care about me - and to feel for the people for whom being alone is their way of life.

There's a guy who camps out at the Metro stop I always take. He looks rough, like he's been on the streets for a long time. Today he was eating part of a pastry and some peas from a can that someone gave him. I always find him sitting there, in that same place. Whenever I see him, he is talking to someone, and people stop to listen to him and then move on.

There are so many people out there like him who need help, like I've never seen before. I want to do a volunteer program sometime after I graduate so I can make a difference. Maybe then, I'll have a better understanding of why I'm here on this earth.

For now, though, I feel at peace, knowing that I can find happiness, no matter where life's road takes me. I realize now that finding happiness is knowing what you want and looking for it at its source – within yourself.

Secrets from My Travel Diaries

➤ *Write down your goals, so you'll know when you've achieved them.*

➤ *Pause to realize how far you've already come.*

➤ *Know what you want, and look for happiness at its source – within yourself.*

CHAPTER 25

One Wild Moment
(United Kingdom, London, Salisbury,
and Stonehenge)

*"I sang along with my Tom Petty tape to the song,
'Time to Move On.' And it was."*

August 4, 1997

All my life, I've heard about England from my grandmother and our relatives who visited us. Ever since that rainy summer day when I was a kid and Mom was watching a special on Princess Diana, I've wanted to see where she lives.

The Hoverspeed (bus-ferry-bus from Paris to London) prices went up because it's summer, but I really want to go, and I'm too close to London not to. I decided to go for it – even though I can't afford to stay more than a few days.

I'm not sure how I'll like traveling by myself. In some ways, I don't feel up for sightseeing again, and now I'll have to find all the places I want to go on my own. My usual traveling partners are already back in the U.S., so there is not much chance of them coming with me. At least I know the language, so that should help.

I decided to call Ryker myself since he never called me. He's out somewhere and hasn't called me back. Who knows if he ever will, but I'll survive either way.

I can't believe I am going to London tomorrow!

August 5, 1997, 10:00 AM

Flying by the seat of my pants, I am now on my way to London. It feels good to be on the "open road" on the highway after riding the metro everywhere in Paris, and hauling around town in Bus 10 in Freiburg.

The bus also has air conditioning, which is a major relief, as I really had to book it to get here and just made it on time. Three travelers with big backpacks arrived as the bus was pulling out, and they got left behind. I guess when they say they're leaving at exactly ten-fifteen in the morning, they truly mean it. Not a lot of things are that way in France.

I was making seven sandwiches (so I could save money in London), getting ready, and packing the last items when the song "You Make a Grown Man Cry" came on the radio. I love that song and hadn't heard it for a long time.

If I hadn't decided to stay and listen to the end of the song, I would have missed Ryker, who called me from work right afterward. Apparently, he had been waiting for me to call him! (He said he couldn't call me back until this morning because when I left the message on his answering machine, I hadn't left my number, and he'd forgotten his address book at the office.)

Unfortunately, Ryker told me that he is leaving on a business trip later this week and won't be back until I'm already gone to Germany. We kept trying to figure out how to see each other again, but there wasn't much we could do. He kept saying he wished he could have called me yesterday, while I kept wishing I didn't have to leave to catch the bus.

For one wild moment, as I was sitting on the metro, I seriously considered changing all my plans to stay in Paris. But I think it's better to just leave things as they are. Deep down, I feel like some of the things I bonded with Ryker about would have ended up being what tore us apart.

At least we had that one wonderful evening together. When I think of kissing him from his perch on the motorcycle on the *rue de la Croix-Nivert,* I feel like doubling over laughing. I had a wonderful time with him that I will remember for a long time.

I don't want to wander around for my whole life, but for now, no one is worth giving up my freedom for. For at least the next few years, I want to come and go as I please, without compromising anything I want to do.

Life is a series of pathways, a cluster of decisions and experiences that have made me who I am. I don't regret what I've done and my decisions because I know that, somehow, I've learned. I've become wiser, stronger, and a better person because of those experiences. I've allowed myself to really live.

It's hard to believe I'll never see Ryker again, though. I can't help but think of him incessantly.

I guess the best remedy for that is to just move on. Go away to some other place where life is a little different. Don't stay where on every corner you hang onto the pieces of the past. Go where you have no corner to remember, no shadows of what you left behind.

I know I'm not yet far enough away from him yet, though, because something in my heart is squeezing me with desperate fingers. The momentum of this bus keeps moving me in a different direction, despite the pulling and tugging on my heart. And so, I continue, further and further away.

August 5, 1997, 4 PM

This road is so bumpy. I can barely write – but really, all I want to do is look out the window, anyway. I can hardly contain myself – I'm on a bus in England!

In a mere two hours from now, I'll be in London. Just the thought of it has excitement scurrying up and down my spine, as if it's the first new place I've ever been.

There was a seemingly endless customs line designated for people from outside of the EU. In front of me in line, a boisterous American guy was asking a finely dressed English lady about her views on the colonies, citing Hong Kong becoming a part of China as an example.

The lady replied that it wasn't talked about in England, but he paid no heed. She politely listened to the guy's opinions the entire time in line. However, she looked like she would have preferred to be just about anywhere else in the world.

The hovercraft trip was turbulent and positively nauseating. I closed my eyes the entire trip so I didn't puke. It was worth it, though, to find myself now speeding down a highway in England.

It's fascinating listening to the conversations behind me. The bus driver called me "Love." I'm realizing that some of the weird English translations I saw on signs in different countries were actually British English expressions – I had no idea!

Just now, I heard someone say "rubbish." I never knew there were people in this world who actually said that in their daily lives! This makes me want to travel all over this part of Europe. I wish Clarissa and Anne were here because this has to be the most fascinating place I have ever been to.

So many things are going on around me; I just want to be a part of it all. After a couple of months of not traveling, I'm reminded of how traveling gets in my blood. If only I could have the chance to lead two lives – one with roots and stability, the other going from one adventure to the next...

I still can't stop thinking of Ryker. I really liked him! I wonder how it would be to have a real relationship with him. I guess I'll never know. I've got to remind myself to stop thinking of him. . .

August 5, 1997, 8:00 p.m.

I'm sitting alone on a random set of stairs leading to the waterway that runs through London. It's quite chilly here, which I wasn't really considering. I should have worn my jeans.

Somehow, I think I'm suffering from culture shock yet again. This place kind of reminds me of home, but also not. I keep telling myself this experience is good for me. I am independent. Still, I miss my friends desperately and wish I knew someone here.

A group of Germans just walked by, which is doing nothing to keep these irrational thoughts from creeping through my head. I can't stop thinking of things that Ryker said to me. With anyone else, the overconfidence would have been really annoying, but from him, it was as if he knew how I felt and understood me.

Should I change my plans to Germany to see him, or just give it a rest? I keep second-guessing my decisions.

What is wrong with me? I have a headache from the craziness of today. It's time to get to bed. I'm so tired of all these thoughts that I can't help but keep thinking.

August 6, 1997 – 9:00 AM

I find myself alone somewhere in England, in some random train station, with no clue exactly where I am. The only thing I know is that at eleven-twenty-one in the morning, I'm getting on another train to go to Salisbury, then taking a bus bound for Stonehenge.

Stonehenge. I'm only going there because Mike and Tom went there and said I shouldn't miss it. However, I don't even have a guidebook, and as much as I think I *should* know, I have no idea what Stonehenge is.

After a morning like this one, I was about ready to throw in the towel on this whole expedition. I have figured out transportation in every other country, but England seems to be marching to the beat of its own drummer.

At six o'clock in the morning, I got up and got ready, only to find that breakfast at the hostel wasn't served until seven-thirty. It was worth waiting for, though, because it was a full breakfast with eggs, beans, potatoes, stewed tomatoes, cereal, croissants, orange juice, and hot chocolate.

I stocked up because I paid dearly for it and want to save my money as much as possible. (It cost me 20 pounds [about $33] to get to Salisbury, and I still have to pay for the bus to Stonehenge!)

Sampling the stewed tomatoes (an acquired taste, I guess), I watched the TV at the breakfast bar. The news was abuzz with updates on Princess Diana, who ironically is not in London, but in Paris. Apparently, she's creating quite a stir, going all around the city with her boyfriend.

"She's met someone who makes her happy at last!" they keep saying on the news. Interesting… I never thought about her being unhappy – I just saw her as a beautiful princess making her mark on the world. . .

After breakfast, I went to Waterloo Station to catch the train, as the guy at the hostel instructed. When it was finally my turn in line at the ticket booth, I discovered it was the wrong station and that I had to go back to Victoria, where I had arrived from yesterday.

I had to ask multiple people where to find the right bus. Finally, I ended up on the right one, but didn't understand what "90 pence" meant and got off at the wrong stop.

Luckily, I asked the driver before he drove away, and he took me back to where I needed to be. I was the only one on the bus, so we talked about where I'd been and even spoke in French. He said he wished he could be mobile like me – and like he was ten years ago when he was 19.

At Victoria Station, I again started in the wrong line, but this time I knew enough to ask the lady in front of me. She gave me directions to the correct ticket counter, but when I got there, I couldn't understand the ticket guy's accent when he told me what platform. (I should have had him write it down for me, but I didn't think of that.)

…Oh, great, it just started to rain. At least I brought my rain jacket, which might help a little…

I ran frantically around the platform. All the trains were about to leave. I asked a couple of people, but no one was of any help.

Finally, I thought I remembered the guys saying something that may have sounded like "12." Impulsively, I ran onto the train on that platform just as the doors were closing.

I got off at the next stop (where I thought the ticket guy told me) and was happy to find "Salisbury" listed on Platform 9. So, I got on that train, but then was confused because Salisbury no longer appeared on the route. Finally, the conductor came by and was very helpful, telling me where to get off and when the next train would arrive to connect me there.

Now, I'm riding backward, through the rain, with people speaking in English accents all around me. I'm hoping I'm getting closer to my destination.

August 6, 1997 – 5:00 PM

I misread the schedule and ended up with a 20-minute wait for my train back to London. My feet are so tired, and I had such a wonderful day, that I don't even care.

On the way back to my hostel, I'm going to stop to see the London Bridge before it gets dark because it's way out of the way of everything else I want to see tomorrow. (Besides, I bought the day pass for the Underground without realizing it, so I might as well use it.)

I thought I was getting sick of traveling, but today I realized that's not really it. I'm sick of traveling to big cities and figuring out where to go. It seems like in London, directions are even harder to figure out.

Usually, the metro is the one form of transportation that I can ride and not get lost. In London, the metro is called the Underground, and it seems to work differently than in the rest of Europe. Each line has a separate name instead of a number, and I can't tell whether I'm going in the right direction.

When I got on the train to Salisbury, I tried writing in my diary, but the guy next to me kept looking over my shoulder, trying to read what I was writing. I found this very distracting, and it continued for a few minutes until a lady walked by and asked where the "Non-Smoking" section was. We looked at each other, confused, then both of us realized at the same instant that we had sat in "Smoking" without knowing it.

That broke the ice, and we ended up talking all the way to Salisbury. He told me he came from a rural part of England. It seemed like he was just as much a fish out of water in London as I was. I guess I can understand why he was confused in London. . . Based on my experience in Salisbury, it's a totally different type of traveling. I think I could wander around towns like that for months without tiring.

During our conversation, he had to ask me to repeat what I said about as many times as I did. I guess neither of us could understand each other's accents too well.

We talked a lot about all the little misunderstandings that happen because of different accents and expressions. I asked him about the long phrase that says "Give Way to Oncoming Vehicles" that appears on the signs here. In the U.S., our sign would simply say "Yield." He said that "Yield" sounded so funny to be on a sign – like something that knights would do.

When I got off the train in Salisbury, a tour to Stonehenge was about to leave, and I hopped on. Now that I know what Stonehenge actually is, I'm amazed.

I cannot fathom ancient people undertaking a project like Stonehenge – I had imagined them merely fighting for survival. There were even sections of stone that used the sun and moon to tell time.

During our free time on the tour, I stopped and watched some birds perched on top of the stones. Oh, to be able to look down at Stonehenge from that view! I thought of how generations of their ancestors had been perched there for thousands of years like birds do everywhere else in the world, but at Stonehenge… What wonder lay beneath!

It's such a strange feeling traveling alone, knowing I can do whatever I want and that no one is waiting for me. I kept thinking I needed to get back to London to meet my friends but then realized I didn't. So, I took my time and wandered around Salisbury. I had only considered it a stopover on the way to Stonehenge, but I soon realized I loved it and spent the rest of the afternoon there.

I loved the tour at the Salisbury Cathedral and listened to the spry older gentleman, with his British humor, for over an hour. At the end of the tour, he told us that one of four remaining copies of the Magna Carta, written on sheepskin in Latin, was right next door. So, for 30 pence, I went to see it.

I can't believe I saw the original basis for Western law in an English town I'd never even heard of, on the way back from seeing an incredible formation that I had no idea what it was before I arrived! Such is traveling by the seat of your pants. . .

August 7, 1997

I was looking at leaflets at the hostel, in the absence of a guidebook, when a Japanese student struck up a conversation with me. She recommended going to the British Museum, which she said is renowned worldwide and has the Rosetta stone. Not only that, but amazingly, the entrance was free.

I seem to keep lucking out like that and have avoided missing all kinds of major attractions in England this way. If I missed anything else, so be it, though, as it would have been impossible to squeeze one more thing in.

Again, the breakfast at the hostel held me over for most of the day, and I had my sandwiches and pretzels for later. I spent about 13 hours running insanely around London.

I stopped first at Saint Paul's Cathedral and Gardens, near my hostel, and then walked along the streets of London to get a feel for the city. Like in Paris, everyone was dressed up, which made me stick out in my T-shirt and jeans shorts – oh, well. I have gotten enough blisters wearing my tennis shoes without trying to dress up, too.

Right when it opened at ten o'clock in the morning, I got to the British Museum, wandered around, and got directions to the Rosetta Stone from one of the guards. The Rosetta Stone was a rather small slab of black rock with writings in three languages. It was a lot less impressive than I'd thought, but the whole concept amazed me.

There was also a section for ancient sculptures and Egyptian mummies, including the giant stone head of Ramesses II. The place was truly amazing, and I would have liked to have stayed for a free guided tour, but I had to get to Buckingham Palace to see the changing of the guard, which started at eleven-thirty in the morning. I battled the crowds and finally got a good vantage point. Their mascot seemed to be a goat for some reason (?).

After that, I went to the ticket booth to inquire about touring Buckingham Palace, only to find that there were no tours that day. The queen had flown out by helicopter to her vacation home in Scotland, so the staterooms weren't open to the public until the next day.

I felt I absolutely could not leave London tomorrow morning without going to Buckingham Palace. So I decided to go to Victoria Station to change my reservations.

As I was making my way along the side of the palace, something that was nothing short of amazing happened. Two people who looked about my age stopped to ask me something. Not really paying attention, I told them I didn't know and was about to speed on by.

They persisted, pursuing me as I kept walking. Finally, I understood they had tickets to the "sneak preview" exhibit at the palace and were trying to find someone to use their extra ticket (?!). I was skeptical and told the guy the exhibit didn't start until the next day.

It turned out he works at Buckingham Palace and had invited his girlfriend to the exhibit, but unexpectedly got tied up with work. So, he wanted to give me his pass for no charge!

Minutes later, I was heading into Buckingham Palace instead of going to the train station, I was heading into Buckingham Palace. She and I presented our passes and went through the series of guards and metal detectors, along with all the other specially invited guests.

We got to see roughly a third of the palace and talked to the guards about each room because there were no guided tours. I particularly enjoyed the music room, where Princess Di had learned to tap dance; the White Room, where there is a trapdoor behind the largest mirror where the queen makes an appearance; and the Bow Room, where the queen gives her annual Christmas speech.

There are no words to describe what it was like to stand in the shadows of past rulers, even the current one who had departed from the garden (where the tour ended) that very morning! Oh, to wear a shimmering dress and make my way through the elaborate Bow Room out to the gardens. In my jeans shorts, I was a far cry from that...

Outside the palace at the end of the tour, we marveled over our intimate experience inside Buckingham Palace, which we shared with only a few guards and invited guests. She told me she and her boyfriend had been standing outside the palace for 10 minutes, trying to find someone to give the ticket to (!). I don't even remember what she said her name was, but she and her boyfriend gave me the most unforgettable gift.

That evening, I returned to my hostel to get ready for my "Aristocratic Pub Walk." (Grandma told me before I left that I should definitely take a walking tour in London, so I really wanted to do that in honor of her.) The walk costs 3.50 pounds (about $6) for students. It was led by another animated jokester, who gave us the inside scoop on the area.

Originally a swampland, Belgravia is now the richest part of London. Famous people like Oscar Wilde, Chopin, and Margaret Thatcher made their homes there. Apparently, it was also where Mozart wrote his first symphony.

We stopped at different pubs, including one where Charles and Diana went on dates, and another on a hidden backstreet where only people who knew about it could find it.

At the very first pub we visited, I met an Italian woman from Milan and a Russian woman who lives in Israel, both professors. We hit it off and ended up walking and talking together for the rest of the tour. All three of us were alone on the tour for different reasons, but we found one another and enjoyed our time so much more. They were so open and full of interesting things to say.

I found the pub walk to be a wonderful way to go out if you're traveling alone – or if you just want to take a piece of London back with you that not everyone knows about.

August 11, 1997

My first trip by myself – and a successful one! I had a positively wonderful time and didn't even mind traveling alone. What Hilda said to me once is true – you can make friends wherever you are.

All in all, I'm really going to miss England. I really love the people and the atmosphere. The many people I talked with and who gave me directions were so helpful and funny. I loved how they would complain in the most dignified fashion while still managing to be convincing that the world had come to an end.

What a society of readers, too. . . On the Underground, absolutely everyone was reading a book, seemingly oblivious to everything else around them. Their timing was impeccable, too.
They'd read until moments before they'd reach their stop, put everything away, and slip out the door in one seamless stroke.

One of the hardest things about being in England was almost getting smashed to oblivion when crossing the street. The sidewalk signs that said "Look Left" or "Look Right" saved me multiple times. The first time I saw the person I thought was a driver not paying attention, I flipped out – until I realized that was the passenger!

Now that I'm back in France, I thought about calling Ryker and leaving a message on his answering machine to say goodbye, but I haven't done it yet. It's funny how only a few days ago I wrote that for "one wild moment" I wanted to stay in Paris to see him.

After all I've experienced in just a few days, it feels like I met him in another lifetime. It's as if he came from another world that I've already left behind…

Secrets from My Travel Diaries

> ➢ *Get a guidebook – but if you do decide to wing it, you meet interesting people and learn unexpected things.*

> ➢ *Don't move so fast that you blow past your VIP ticket.*

> ➢ *Figure out which way to look.*

CHAPTER 26

Ich bin satt. [I'm full.]
(Paris to Wittenberg)

"My circumstances seem to change daily, but that no longer bothers me. I make a plan and then just stay open to what life has to offer."

August 13, 1997

I should be packing and cleaning John's apartment, but despite my good intentions, I haven't done anything. Today I went to *Le Tex-Mex*, *la rue de la Croix-Nivert*, and *le Champs de Mars* to take pictures of the places where I'd "found myself," I guess you could say. Once I got to the park, my usual bench called to me. The weather is beautiful, so here I am, soaking everything in and saying goodbye to this part of my life.

There are so many things about Paris that I'll really miss. I love the excitement that I feel all around me. In fact, that is what first drew me here. I'm so glad I've come because I've discovered the city and myself in ways I never knew.

The idea of leaving makes me incredibly sad and a little scared. I can't imagine not being in Europe any longer. I've come to love being here. I love just being different. And I'll miss speaking French.

At the same time, I'm looking forward to being home again. Soon, I'll be leaving with nothing but memories. My entire life is in this diary and the others I carry with me. To add anything else would be too complicated for now.

August 15, 1997

After a bit of haggling, frantic packing, and a lot of pulling and tugging on my suitcase, I am set to take the train to Germany tomorrow.

I went to the *Bahnhof* [train station] (which will always be the *Bahnhof*, even though I know that here it's called the *gare*) to secure a place on the train. Going to Germany on a fast train is expensive. I decided to save almost $100 by taking a train to the border of Germany instead and then picking up a weekend ticket, valid for unlimited train rides all over the country.

Saving the money is worth it, but I can see myself going a little insane with that long, slow ride, which will take all day and into the evening. Luckily, I have four romance novels in my suitcase to keep me busy on the trains, and there's always my diary, my constant companion.

I wish I still had my Eurail pass, but oh, well. It seems that every time I plan how much something will cost, it's always a lot more, like shipping my suitcase home, buying my train ticket, and taking the trip to London. I'd better get out of Europe before I'm totally broke.

August 16, 1997

My hands are caked with filth as they grip this pen, my clothes reeking of dried sweat. I've had to change trains six times in random cities, and I've finally made it to the last leg of the trip. It was incredibly hot today, and lugging four small bags around is such a pain.

I keep wondering what I can leave behind but haven't come up with much yet. I already shipped the bigger suitcase back because it was filled to the brim with things I can live without for now, and it tips over even more often than the smaller one.

It has been a random ride, with people getting on and off constantly. One lady hopped on carrying only a watering can and hopped off a couple of stops later.

On the first train, there were swarms of people. I stood on the moving train, reading a romance novel in French that I'd picked up in Paris, and noticed the other passengers eying me curiously. I guess I looked a little out of place: reading a book in French, wearing my Hard Rock Café Orlando shirt, and eating a German muesli granola bar with my handbag still sporting the Dover tags from my trip to England.

The passenger standing next to me started up a conversation with me in French, asking where I was from and where I was headed. Everyone leaned in and listened with curiosity.

By the second connection, I'd figured out how to get all geared up early so I could be ready to get off in time with all my baggage. I didn't have too many problems, except when there were no escalators, which there never are in the small *Bahnhöfe* [train stations].

Now, I'm sitting on the ground waiting for my next train because there are only a few benches, and they are already full. I miss England, where there were private waiting rooms by each *Gleis* [track] that even had restrooms. Then again, I don't miss the English prices, so I'll deal with it.

I forgot to pack water, so I have nothing to drink and can find nothing on this *Gleis*. Even though I have half an hour of waiting time, the idea of unnecessarily going up and down the stairs keeps me from going.

I'm still recovering from my last connection. I only had five minutes to change trains, which made me nervous; then, to top it off, my train arrived late, and there was no escalator. Luckily, the next train was late, so I was just able to make the connection. (Missing it would have thrown off my complicated schedule – I don't even want to think about that.)

When the next connection came only minutes later, I felt like I was going to pass out from exhaustion and thirst. I was completely deflated and struggled to muster the energy to keep going. Finally, I dragged myself to my usual spot by the doors.

As I was standing there, someone offered to help, which I gratefully accepted. He carried my suitcase all the way to the next train (even though it's so much easier to wheel it), shook my hand, and asked in a concerned way if I'd be all right, alone with my bags. I told him I would and thanked him.

It's still not easy being alone, despite how infinitely more independent I've become. But the help of kind strangers gets me through.

We passed by a sign that said Düsseldorf, and I couldn't help but wonder where Ryker's other apartment in Düsseldorf is. I know he'll be arriving back in Paris tonight or tomorrow morning. By then, I'll be far away.

I think it's ironic how I met no actual *Freiburgers* while I was in Freiburg, but came to Paris to meet one.

I was just reading the entry from when I first came to London, with my head full of thoughts of him.

Sigh. . .

We are finally – I almost dare not believe it – coasting into Lutherstadt Wittenberg.

August 17, 1997

The lowest point of the entire trip was when I arrived. I managed to haul my luggage to a phone booth, only to find out that my card only had 20 *Pfennige* [pennies]. I tried to dial up the Müllers anyway, but the phone just rang and rang, and the next time I put the card in, it flashed *ungültig* [invalid].

Next, I lugged all my bags to the bathroom – only to find out I didn't have a 50 *Pfennig* coin to put in the door slot. I was about to go into the shop to buy a phone card, but the lady locked the place and left as I approached. I had no choice but to spend 15 deutsche marks [about $9] on a cab.

As it turned out, I'd written down the wrong phone number. Everyone was home and surprised to see me when I showed up at their door, dirty, exhausted, and hauling my four bags.

We had a late dinner and talked for a long time. When we finally turned in, I was so tired I could barely even string together a sentence.

So, here I am, in familiar Wittenberg. If it weren't so hot here, and if I weren't so exhausted, sore, and incredibly thirsty, I'm sure things would look much better.

August 20, 1997

I've gone from this diary being my only friend, to being around people constantly. It is really an adjustment, but one that's fun to make – as much as I enjoyed the independent world that I created for myself in Paris.

Today Nadine and I biked through a wooded path to a tucked-away lake. We spent the afternoon swimming in the lake and talking about our hopes and dreams. Nadine said I speak German so well now and don't even sound

American. I don't know about that, but speaking German is much more automatic now.

It was so wonderful and refreshing to be there. The weather was very hot, and the water felt so cool. In fact, this was the first time it felt like summer this whole year. I prefer city life over the longer term, but I also really enjoy being out in the country. Life seems so much simpler. It's a wonderful escape to be able to relax for a while.

My upcoming return to the U.S. looms in the background all the time. When I got to the Müllers' house, a letter from Clarissa was waiting for me. She said it was strange being home at first, but she'd adjusted quickly. Hopefully, it will be equally easy for me.

August 22, 1997

I was reading a book to Katrin this morning. She's only five years old and can't read, but she always listens intently and corrects my German. It's amazing how she automatically knows genders and plurals in a way that I will never match.

Katrin was excited about the new kitty they were bringing home and asked me for advice on the name. I told her that many cats in America are named Fluffy, and the name stuck. It was hilarious to see the whole family calling, "Fluffy!" in a German accent as they tried to coax the cat out of its hiding place to take it home with us.

This afternoon was so extremely hot. I biked into the city alone and sat for hours in the shade on a bench by the Martin Luther *Denkmal* [Monument]. The shadows of myself and Clarissa, from when we studied here two years ago, whispered to me at every corner. It's the first time I've been here without her.

Everyone in the group who studied in Freiburg has gone home now, except for me. In six days, I, too, will take the flight across the ocean and close this chapter of my life. Sometimes, just the thought of it consumes my entire being.

There's no use hanging on, though. Life will go on whether I'm in Europe or anywhere else. I just have to *genießen* this time as much as I can. (How I love the connotation of that word, which perfectly describes the past six months. If only there were a good translation in English! The closest I could come would take a couple of words, like "thoroughly enjoy." That just doesn't capture the same essence, though.)

Mom called just as I was about to go to bed. Everything has fallen into place for my return home. Afterward, I was filled up with the wonderful feeling of home I always have when talking with her.

I feel like I'm trapped between two worlds. . . I'm close to moving on again, but this time I'm heading the opposite way across the Atlantic.

Two years ago, when I was reluctantly leaving Germany the last time, I remember Renata telling me, *"Dein Zuhause ist auch schön"* ["Your home is also beautiful"]. This time, I realize how poignantly true that really is.

Sitting side by side on the plane six months ago, Clarissa and I clutched each other's hands and said goodbye to the U.S. We said we had to look closely down at it because we were leaving it for a very long time.

Now I realize that I needed to fly away from my homeland and the life it holds for me so that I could see it more clearly. When I fly back into my life in the U.S. again, I know it will be with an entirely different perspective.

When I step off the plane in America, never will I have been so incredibly broke nor so incredibly fulfilled. I've done everything I set out to do. It is time for a new adventure to begin. But instead of in France or Germany, the next one will be in the United States of America.

My days of lugging my bags on and off trains by myself are officially over now. Renata has arranged for me to ride to the Frankfurt airport with her friends, who will take me there in their car.

I will miss the freedom of getting on a train and going wherever I have the mind to go. But it will also be nice to get in a car when I want to, without worrying about the day or time.

August 24, 1997

I'm nearly done packing, which is a tremendous relief. I don't like packing, as much as I've always loved going places. I wish I could just fold up my closet and set it back up again wherever in the world I find myself. It would make my life infinitely easier.

When I unpacked when I first got here, there was a total explosion of loose articles all over the floor, and I had difficulty finding anything. So, I thought this time I'd start early to get everything tamed and back into the suitcase.

After much effort, I stuffed in every ounce of what would fit inside, and the suitcase zipped. Now that it's done, I plan to live out of my big backpack until I go home.

Home. It feels so far away now, but soon it will be so near. In some ways, I can't wait, but in other ways, I can't let go of everything I've built around me. I guess that's why I felt lost in my own world today and couldn't pull myself out.

Here I am, filling up the last page of this diary. When I started it, it found me on the brink of a new adventure in Paris. Then, it accompanied me all through

Paris, England, and back in Germany, where I'm comfortably visiting the dear people I've come to know and enjoy.

On the pages of this diary, I have strung together so many words to describe all that has happened and all that has gone through my head. As I write the last words it will hold, I'm about to begin another chapter of my life. In two days, I'm heading back where I started.

So many thoughts come to my mind now. I've grown so much during these past six months *et des poussieres* [and a bit], as they say in French. I will hold the riches of those incredible times in my heart for the rest of my life.

I also know there is more out there for me to experience in life, though. When I return to the U.S., I will start saving up again so that I can take another adventure away from home. Everything I've done to get right here, right now, has been worth it. The money I saved for so many months before I came here bought me freedom, mobility, and some of the best times in my life. I want that again.

My grandparents lived through the Depression and taught me to save money instead of spending it. I'm inclined to find a different balance between saving and spending now. I'd like not just to save, but also to fill my life with the fireworks of adventures and brightly colored memories. There comes a point when you have to realize you can't take it with you.

I went over to see Renata, and we talked for a long time. She said she admired my affinity for writing things down. Sometimes, she said, she wonders what she's done with the past 50 years of her life.

Maybe with the help of all the diaries I've filled up, I won't have to wonder. I can always just look back and make sense of all that stretches behind.

August 25, 1997

The Müllers and I went to a movie tonight. I was surprised that Günther wanted to talk after we got back, even though it was already ten-thirty at night, which is when he usually goes to bed.

Never in the times I've talked with him have I had such a portal into his heart and mind as I had tonight. I was really struck by his confession about his son Tobias's weeklong vacation at the grandparents'. He said he was happy Tobias was doing so well, but at the same time had a nagging feeling that he's already losing his son after only nine years.

Günther also remarked that he was sure my dad felt the same way about me. I know it's true, too, because I got chills when he said it.

Eight years after the Berlin Wall came down, the impacts are still unfolding. Now, he said, it's difficult to travel anywhere, even to places that used to be easy for them to go, like Russia and some of the other eastern countries. He talked about having to push his passport under a window where he couldn't see the receiver of it, and about waiting and wondering if he'd ever see it again.

Even for American students, traveling through Eastern Europe still entails constantly getting off the train to show your passport at random stops. All that will change over time, but he made me appreciate even more the significance of what I've been able to do. I am freer than anyone of that generation could have imagined.

It's also significant that I am the first American that Günther has ever gotten to know. For so long, America was a forbidden and perhaps even fairytale-like place. Now, he said, I am an example for him. I represent what is to come for his own children, who are growing up in a different world than he did. Perhaps they may even do what I did and live in a foreign land, something he could never have fathomed.

After Günther went to bed, I couldn't sleep. Instead, I stayed up listening to *Wildflowers*, just thinking about how blessed I am to be so free to go where I please.

At last, I am beginning to be sure it truly is time to go home. I'm bursting at the seams with my experiences and couldn't ask for anything more. As Günther said, I've experienced so much and am now *satt* [full].

Through all these experiences, I'm not convinced that there is anything I truly could *not* do if I really wanted to. It's a very comforting, secure feeling, and it's been hard-won.

As I sit here in the wee hours of the morning, I am overtaken by an eerie sensation of realizing, in a whole new way, how precious this adventure has really been. I feel almost unworthy of the magnitude of what I've been able to experience. Never in my life have I felt so blessed – and so incredibly free.

Secrets from My Travel Diaries

➢ *Pay to upgrade to the fast train, if you can.*

➢ *Fill your life with the fireworks of adventures and brightly colored memories.*

➢ *Know when you're full, and be grateful.*

CHAPTER 27

The Journey Comes Full Circle

"There are so many dreams yet unrealized for me – but I
also know I'll never have this dream again."

August 27, 1997

This is my last day in Germany. I have no idea what to think or feel. I think I'm in shock. Classes have already started at home, and I'm still hanging on to the last minutes of my European adventure.

It's time to let go of the beautiful dream I've been living for so long. I've done everything I set out to do.

I'm about to swoop down in my homeland again, and I will start my internship shortly after I get back.

I'm flying back to my life once again.

August 28, 1997

I am on the plane, waiting to take off. Soon, I will cross the ocean back to where I started.

...I had only written those two sentences before the lady beside me started a conversation. I had forgotten how people randomly talk to you all the time in the U.S. It first struck me on the transit bus to the plane, where strangers were laughing and conversing. There would be silence on a bus with only Germans, with only occasional quiet conversation between people who already knew one another.

Anyway, yesterday on the *Autobahn* with Renata's friends Emma and Otto, "Born in the USA" came on, and I felt my heart swell with pride as I thought of my country. The U.S. has its problems, but it will always be home. As much as I love Europe, I will always have the American way of life running through my veins.

Last night was a very odd night. I kept having strange dreams of coming home, like one in which my dad had an earring and wasn't enthusiastic about seeing me. The dreams continued through the night, and I was sound asleep when Emma woke me up for my last German breakfast.

I don't think it's hit me that I'm leaving Europe, after changing countries so many times. This time I'm on a plane headed across the ocean, instead of taking a train.

We left for the airport and ate at McDonald's, where I had my last *Gemüse Mac [Veggie Mac]*. It was a bit ironic that my last meal in Germany was at McDonald's, but it was the only restaurant open. Emma and Otto said it was good *Vorbereitung* [preparation] for America.

They couldn't go any further since they weren't ticketed passengers, so we said goodbye before I went through the metal detectors. Shortly after, I boarded the plane. I so need a break from suitcases and goodbyes. I hugged Emma and Otto, and they wished me *Alles gute* [All the best]. Now, I'm once again *unterwegs* [en route], this time headed back across the Atlantic.

In some ways, I don't want to go back; in other ways, I do. It's time for life to go on and for me to pick up where I left off, a bit older and much wiser. My interlude of sailing away wherever I want needs to end for now. It's time to head back to the real world.

I came to Freiburg with only a scant understanding of who I was and full of questions I didn't even know to ask. Then, in discovering new questions, everything I thought I knew got all changed around and confused. It wasn't until I found myself in Paris that I put the puzzle pieces back together again.

I'm filled by this incredible experience but have not changed to the point of being unrecognizable to the people I care about. My eyes are open a lot wider now, but I still have the same sense of humor and smile.

Ultimately, I'm glad for my decisions and for how things have worked out all around. Life is a mystery because you never know what's around the corner.

…I just laid eyes on what I think was U.S. soil. It's been more than half a year since I've seen my homeland. I remember my last glimpse of it so clearly. I will never be that person again.

It's officially time now, to close the most amazing chapter in my 21 years. It gives me physical pain when I think of all I will no longer see and experience as part of my daily life. I still find myself thinking in German, but now, no one around me will understand. That will be hard to get used to.

I feel a weight across my chest as I look out the window. I keep listening to the first four songs of *Wildflowers* over and over again.

I have so many dreams yet unrealized, but I also know I'll never have this dream again. Knowing this makes me want to cling to the last minutes, but they're already gone. They're figments of the past that I'll never forget. In an uncertain world, that much is certain.

One thing I do know, though, is that my heart, mind, and very self are filled to the brim with all the wonder I've absorbed, all the dreams I've chased, and all the adventures that I've had.

Never in my wildest dreams could I have imagined, when I got on the plane to cross the Atlantic, how all my dreams – and so much more – could be fulfilled. I will hold these incredible times in my heart for the rest of my days.

Secrets from My Travel Diaries

➢ *Hold your memories in your heart… But let go of the excess baggage.*

➢ *Reignite the Adventurer within, and realize your wildest dreams.*

➢ *Set yourself free.*

CHAPTER 28

Set Yourself Free

"At 21, I'm embarking on a journey to figure out who I am and to bask in the joy of being young and so alive. I truly hope these next six months will shape the rest of my life and that these moments will age into memories that I will cherish for a lifetime." - 1997

March 1, 2023

It is so surreal how the memories I forgot come back clear as day as I read, Anne said.

I'm up early, reading her text. These past few weeks of editing of this manuscript have been intense. Anne, Clarissa, and I have been on a group chat every day. It is bringing us together again and erasing the passage of time.

What started as a phantom character, a thought and dream, and a search bar that didn't return a name has become... *this.*

Your book is like historical fiction now, Clarissa texted.

Like so much that I only now realize is so true.

Now, my phone tells me where to go… my favorite music plays on demand… I take as many pictures as I want and delete the ones I don't… And when I meet someone, I text them and follow them on social media.

I don't process my experiences by creating a paper scrapbook anymore. Why should I? My phone makes those itself; I don't even have to ask. It sends me an alert, and the memories come with music accompaniment.

Everything is so much easier now… but it's also not.

There was no built-in device to slow down, appreciate, and understand where I've been – and where I'm going…

Until I found my diaries.

Taking the time to read them – and read them again – spiraled me into a tsunami of understanding
Who I am…
What my life is about…
The choices I've made (or made by default)…

They've given me answers.

What was it about Ryker that so piqued my curiosity? I remember vividly that moment of stepping back, as we went through the turnstiles on the metro. It's eerie. *Why?*

At 30 years old, Ryker was living a life I had never imagined. He fascinated and scared me at the same time.

And he also called my bluff. He zeroed in so quickly on what no one else had seen.

As he said, I had a vision of the near term, but the longer term was hazy. I wanted to be an independent, successful career woman with an international career and family. But I couldn't really see it. I was brought up in a completely different way, with no real example to shape that vision.

I knew what I wanted – and was told I could have it. Yet, without knowing it, I was following a deeply ingrained and incongruent script. And under that wiring, stepping back to let him lead was automatic.

As a kid, I remember going on a week-long vacation to a cottage in Michigan. Dad had taken the top off the car for the summer, and we were ready to go.

My dad was like Superman to me. He would swoop in after work, and the fun would begin. Meanwhile, Mom was always in the background, making everything work behind the scenes. For years, I didn't understand the role she played. She was just always there for us.

Dad was running late from work that day. I remember being disappointed and even bewildered by it.

He had a stable job in his company's engineering department, and his hours were usually predictable. But he'd gotten a promotion into management, which shifted his responsibilities. I didn't grasp that concept until years later.

We waited and waited. It seemed like an eternity.

Meanwhile, everything was packed in our red Jeep, impeccably organized. Only Mom had any idea what we were even taking with us. The rest of us didn't even give it a thought. She always had it covered.

Finally, after what seemed like an eternity, Dad pulled hurriedly into the driveway, stressed... frustrated... distracted. My brother and I looked at Mom hopefully.

She shook her head. "Your father still needs to do his workout."

My dad always worked out – six days a week. He didn't miss his workouts for pretty much anything.

And so, we waited while he did his full workout – every last rep.

When we were almost ready to go, Mom got my brother and me into the Jeep. All three of us sat there, like supporting actors, staged and ready… waiting for the lead to show up.

At last, he appeared, lean, fit, and fresh from the shower. The keys were already dangling in the ignition. All he had to do was turn the key.

He swooped into the driver's seat, and we were off. Mom had done everything else, but he was the superhero to me. He was the one who whisked us away.

This was how I grew up. Simple. Clear. We knew exactly who was in charge and what role each of us had to play. The vision we followed was largely my dad's. Mom bought into it and was always there to make it happen – but there was no question about who the primary creator was.

I was so blessed to have a childhood with two wonderful parents. But it didn't prepare me to navigate the world I would live in – a world of dual careers, big cities, and new rules.

It's taken until now to realize that later, with my own family, I was trying to occupy not one – but two – seats in that Jeep. In my vision, I was in the driver's seat, swooping in and turning the ignition. And, following Mom's script without even knowing it, I was the one riding in the front passenger seat, keeping my family together and organized, too.

And here's where the plot thickens. There was a third role at play. It was that of the man who would swoop in with all the answers and whisk me away to where I wouldn't have a care in the world. Instead of doing that, though, Ryker left me with more confusion. His world, at the time, was too different for me to be able to connect the dots.

So, I did instead what was certain to bring adventure and fun. I caught another wave and then another. I ran all over London, connected from train to train back to Germany. I returned to the U.S., kept doing it all, and lived out the vision in which the sole creator was me.

Eventually, my life mirrored looking out at the Eiffel Tower as it cast a light across the city. Living on the surface, I lost the richness of standing underneath.

Time slid by, like water flowing to wherever it could make a path. I never slowed down long enough to realize I didn't know where I was going. I just kept going.

Once you get caught up in the rolling waves, changing course is not easy. But I got to a point where I could no longer ignore the whispers that there was something more. I began to use the long plane rides on business trips worldwide to read and reflect.

I began to invest in myself and in finding answers. At a weekend workshop, I met entrepreneurs operating at the highest level – entrepreneurs from all over the world. I was floored by their way of thinking and their perspective of possibility and abundance.

Taking furious notes the whole time, I learned morning rituals and new ways of doing and thinking. In the following months, I invested in myself further, implemented what I'd learned – and began to see and move through the world in an entirely different way.

In reconnecting with who I once was, I realized I'd been pushing my true self – and the dreams that lit me up – down for years. I began to write again, after laying my writing aside for more than ten years.

The parts of me that had gotten buried started to reemerge. I stopped resisting what I knew deep down inside and gained the courage to show up as who I am instead of blending in and pleasing others.

After years of feeling lost at sea, I got clarity in my life. And I learned how differently I could navigate, knowing who I was, what I wanted, and why I wanted it. Finding those answers has changed everything in my life.

When I began to let myself shine, people noticed that I looked different, felt different, and moved differently through the world. They wanted to know how I did and started to say, "I'll have what she's having." (Remember *When Harry Met Sally?*)

I joined masterminds and began coaching clients on how to do what I did… Find their purpose… Monetize their passion… Step into freedom.

I started Wind In Your Sails Consulting.

And I set myself free.

"You Can Have It All" and "You Can Do It All" were like an oasis, always "out there" on the horizon. I was speeding through life, never reaching my destination, because "You can do anything" and "You can have it all" – and still get nowhere.

They were like a formula with a circular reference. . . a bridge that doesn't go all the way across. I never defined what "it" was, so I was left with no milestones to celebrate. The other side of the next big wave, and the next, led only to a vast, empty ocean.

Wave after wave trapped me in an endless spiral and became their own means to an end. They got me so stuck in the "what" – that I forgot to ask *why*. That, I've realized, is inevitably where chasing "it all" leads.

I was so caught up in the next wave coming my way that I didn't know I'd lost my compass – and the lighthouses to guide me along the way. Just bailing water, I was struggling to stay afloat. The open horizon of possibility stretched before me, but I stopped seeing it.

My 21-year-old self, my mentor, with the words she wrote in multi-colored pens... She's taught me a lot. But I wouldn't be here unless I'd already made the choice. I wouldn't be right here, right now, if I hadn't chosen to seek out those diaries in the first place, write my story, and own what was on the pages.

On vacation last summer, my sister-in-law and I were out dancing at the beach. The band played "I Wanna Dance with Somebody." The song struck a chord, taking me back in time once again. I remember playing that Whitney Houston tape over and over in high school.

The energy intensified in the room as we all danced and sang. And I could feel the shared bond with these women I'd never met. It was nostalgia for a simpler time when the canvas was nearly blank – when it felt like anything was possible.

Back then, I guess all we really wanted was to dance with someone who would sweep us away. It all seemed so simple then, so much simpler than it turned out to be – even for Whitney herself.

So, where does that leave us now? I still believe you can have it all, do anything you set your mind to, and have a love that lasts. But I've also learned there's no "standard" definition for what that means. You have to define and redefine it yourself, as the chapters in your life are written.

At 21, I thought "finding yourself" was a task you completed, like checking something off your "to-do" List. So, when I got off the plane back in the U.S., I considered "finding myself" complete. And I continued with my life.

But the tides of life kept shifting. And I didn't know that finding new answers – finding my Truth – required fresh intentionality.

But now I do.

And now, at last, the clarity of my vision and purpose has set me free.

Those last lines in my diary on August 28, 1997, were my ride-off-into-the-sunset moment. They were the crescendo with the inspirational music right, before the credits rolled. But real life doesn't work that way.

Life kept meandering on. I spent years wading through everything I thought I "should" or "had to" do, waiting for the next crescendo. But that next crescendo was waiting for me... To move beyond decades past and create a *shared* vision with my family... To take the helm... To chart my own course... To find my compass and set sail on the open seas...

Now, each day is a precious gift – an empty canvas, yet to be painted. After anything that I desire to do but haven't done, I place a "yet" after it.

I consider that "yet," nothing more than a chapter yet to be written. And I know that I can write that chapter however I want.

"Tomorrow is promised to no one," Mom told me again and again in the two years of suffering from pancreatic cancer before she passed away. She was right.

And that quote about how twenty years later, you regret the things you didn't do more than the things you did? That, I can also confirm, is true. So now, I'm remembering again that I'm finished with regrets.

Chasing my dreams, I feel like I'm jumping off that mountain in the Alps. But just when I start to fear losing my camera, the wind catches my parachute, and I rediscover why the birds sing.

"Never again will you be this free" gave me only temporary permission to be free. But setting myself free doesn't have to end.

In many ways, "Never again will you be this free" made 1997 what it was. It heightened the sense of adventure and the importance of those times. It carried with it an urgency to really live the moment.

But after that, 1997 became a mountain I could never climb again… A time in my life for which nothing could compare… A yearning for something that could never be again.

So, right here, right now, I choose to own the thoughts in my head – and the words I wrote on trains, on benches, and after nights out with my friends.

I choose to jump off that mountain and glide through the air, to release these words and make my "tiny mark on the world."

I choose to own every twist and turn in my life… Every success and every failure… Every chance I took, and every time I sat on the shoreline and watched and waited instead.

Right here, right now, I'm calling this a pivotal moment. I'm going to play my "ever after" music and ride off into the sunset once again.

And tomorrow, I'll begin again – different, but not the same.

Because I'm not starting from the beginning – I'm starting from what I know to be true.

I know now that life is messy. It's so much messier than I ever imagined that day on the plane.

Life meandered to so many places I didn't expect... But I choose to keep sailing anyway – and let go of what has served its purpose.

Right here, right now, I choose to let go of 1997. To no longer stand in the shadow of it.

I release it... to *you*... so that in it, you will find your own Truth.

Because on the horizon is... Freedom.

The choice to stand at the precipice of possibility.

To let go of what is holding you back and make your own rules.

To step out from the illusion of limitation. Into the light of clarity. Into *your* Truth.

This is *your* time to take the helm, let the wind fill up your sails, and go where only you can go.

Remove the "Never again will you" and just "Feel this free."

Your music is playing. I'm extending you a rose. It's time to "Discover why the birds sing."

Reignite your Adventurer within.

Set yourself free.

Secrets from My Travel Diaries

> ➤ *Clarity is knowing who you are, where you're going – and who and where you are not.*

Acknowledgments

I am incredibly grateful to the people in my life who have supported me on the incredible unfolding of writing this book.

I'd like to especially thank:

- ❖ My husband, David, for believing in me.
- ❖ Celeste and Stephen for inspiring me every day.
- ❖ Dad and Scott for understanding what it is to dream of being an author.
- ❖ Heather Bodle and Sara Bock, for being in the Google doc and everywhere I needed you… you know how much this means!
- ❖ Marion Gammill-Keller, for being with me all along.
- ❖ Pam Schindler, for declaring me a Marketer from the beginning.
- ❖ David Barry, DeAnn Christensen, Ricardo Fiorillo, Stacy Jackson-Williams, and Joe Mikels, for your insights and support on my many drafts.
- ❖ Marta Bourke, Kathy Kirby, and Sherry Martin for sisterhood through it all.
- ❖ Natasha Klages, for knowing what my book was about more than I did.
- ❖ Rikin Patel, Ayda Sabri, Dunia Hamdi, and the Titans for showing me a whole new way.
- ❖ Uncle Jeff, Aunt Barb, Uncle Mark, Aunt Kathe, Aunt Joyce, and Uncle Dale for your love and mentorship.

- ❖ Jamie Fisher Wintz and Kendra Priest for being the sisters I never had.
- ❖ Donna Priest, for loving my stories, and Ray Priest for sharing so many of yours.
- ❖ Jennifer Fondrevay for modeling the "how."
- ❖ Lanay Johns, for going live in the wrong place and everything thereafter.
- ❖ Jenny Sälgeback and Anne Sluhan for yellow flowers and swan boats.
- ❖ Chasity Grant, for calling me out - and being ready to receive.
- ❖ Larisa Olteanu, for encouraging me to go big.
- ❖ Dr. Kevin Keyes, for keeping me in alignment.
- ❖ Becky Skillin, for your pages of questions and suggestions that kept me going deeper.
- ❖ Bree Kidd-Taylor, because we never knew all the places your photos would end up.
- ❖ Stacy Harris, Angela Aja, and Kinsey Machos for sharing your expertise.
- ❖ The Woodlands Chamber of Commerce, NIA, MCABW, the Friday Coffee Connection, and TBirds around the world, for making me feel like coming home.
- ❖ Adriana Wells, because it must have been you in my bunk in Budapest.
- ❖ Wittenberg University, IES Abroad, Kappa Delta Sorority, and Thunderbird School of Global Management for the incredible experiences you provided.
- ❖ Cris Cawley and the team at Game Changer Publishing for making my dream your project.
- ❖ Cheryl Strayed, for inspiring me to write what was in my heart, no matter when.
- ❖ Robin Sharma, Tony Robbins, and Dean Graziosi for selling me on investing in my dreams.

THANK YOU FOR READING MY BOOK!

DOWNLOAD YOUR FREE GIFTS

Just to say thanks for buying and reading my book, I would like to give you a few free bonus gifts, no strings attached!

To Download Now, Visit:

http://Igniteyouradventurer.com/bookfreegifts

I appreciate your interest in my book, and value your feedback as it helps me improve future versions. I would appreciate it if you could leave your invaluable review on Amazon.com with your feedback. Thank you!

Made in the USA
Monee, IL
12 July 2023

39074061R00187